Going Soul-o:

A Tale of Personal Transformation

Heather Tweddle

First published in 2010 by
Heather Tweddle

CIP catalogue records for this book are available
from The British Library.

ISBN 978-0-9567047-0-2

CHANDLER® BOOK DESIGN

Cover design and typeset by Chandler Book Design,
www.chandlerbookdesign.co.uk

Printed in Great Britain by
Ashford Colour Press Ltd.

Become

Who

You

Were

Born

To

Be

Contents

For

Neil Tweddle
and
Bryce Taylor

Acknowledgements

The existence of this book owes much to the many people who have had a profound impact upon my life during the last 19 years: those who travelled alongside me through the pain of sudden bereavement; those who enabled me to discover other paths and stayed with me as I stepped into the unknown; those with whom I could share some of my journey; those with whom I still share new insights, new experiences, new understandings; those who have contributed to this work, particularly the critical friends who have lovingly read and commented upon it in its formation. To all of them I express my heartfelt thanks.

The author 'at home' in the mountains of Machu Picchu

Introduction

"Live in your Bliss." **Joseph Campbell**

The inspiration and material for this book is deeply rooted in my own awakening to the spiritual dimension of my life and the journey that has, and still is, leading me along. It is a path with many corners, many cliff faces, many wonderful still moments and many joys, challenges, people and steps to be taken. What brought me to writing this account was the desire to describe the learning, the perspectives and the insights I have gained; learning that has only come through my experiences.

On the spiritual path, following existing traditions cannot be sustained without personal experiences, yet being open to, accepting and trusting our own experiences often brings us into conflict with those traditional beliefs. This is something I have lived; I have lived the dilemmas and challenges that come from being within a strong tradition yet feeling the need to step outside it[1]. I know that being part of the Church was a crucial and necessary stepping stone for me but, in time, I also knew I needed to step outside it. I gave up faith for experience: living through the conflict and living out the conflict was hugely difficult.

---

[1] My journey through the Church and beyond is described in *Chapter 4 The Pathless Path: Entering the Forest.*

This book describes and explores the key phases I have travelled through thus far. There was my awakening to the possibilities of the journey (*Chapter 1 Awakening: Coming Alive*), followed by the clearing of my intra- and inter-personal 'stuff' (*Chapter 2 Travelling into the Shadowlands*) in order to gain the spaciousness and inner freedom (*Chapter 3 Walking in Freedom*) to claim my journey and step fully and consciously into the spiritual dimension (*Chapter 4 The Pathless Path: Entering the Forest*). Along the way I encountered more and more non-ordinary states and other beings of a kind I could never have predicted or imagined and these are described in *Chapter 5 Wild Encounters*.

As part of my developing awareness and attention I knew it was imperative I found ways of bringing my learning to living in the world as well as facing and acknowledging the implications and consequences of my journey; this is the focus of *Chapter 6 Being in the World*. Throughout my shifts and changes I was always looking to find the ways that fit for me to enhance my awareness, my levels of consciousness and fulfil my potential. *Chapter 7 Inspirations and Influences* thus looks at the many activities, approaches and strategies that have inspired and influenced me as I have travelled my path, many of which remain important and still inform my practice.

Chapter 8 Healing through Meeting is the final chapter of the book because it is, for me, arguably the most critical of all the dimensions of my journey. Without the people I met in various ways and with various roles I know my journey would have been tremendously less rich than it has been. I also know that without them and their meetings with me my journey would not have progressed in the way it has; the healing I have experienced from people along the way was and will always be crucial, joyous, liberating, challenging and of value without measure.

I positively encourage the reader to use this book in whatever way they choose, and encouragement, too, not to get hung up on being in any one place, or order of events, or expected 'progress' or sequence in your journey. My book also comes with a 'health warning' because change and challenge will be there simply by being willing to enter into some form of dialogue with yourself, with the spiritual dimension of your life. The book recognises a *living* spirituality which means having to work on personal blocks and patterns, and with interpersonal difficulties.

I believe this form of exploration and discovery is a vital part of the times in which we live. Many people yearn to find meaning in their lives and seek, through all manner of channels, to find their own path and their own purpose. The world truly is ripe, and almost desperate, for a spiritual thread to existence and yet many are also afraid to take up the challenge or just do not know where to start.

I've met many dangers – physical as well as emotional and spiritual – on my journey so I can give some assurance and confidence, offering key points, signposts and markers, to others. So my hope is that this book will contribute towards others finding **their** path and that it will play a part in enabling them to find their way to becoming who they truly are born to be: to become more free and confident in the path they have chosen as the unique, sacred beings they are.

1

Awakening: Coming Alive

"May you awaken to the vision that inspires you; may your heart be guided by love; and your mind by divine wisdom that all things may find a better way."

Frances Vaughan, *The Inward Arc*, p28, Shambala, 2000.

Introduction

The idea of travelling to other parts of the world offers the prospect of exploration, of discovery, of seeing and visiting new places, of learning, of meeting new people and experiencing new things. All of these have proved equally applicable to a journey of a different kind – my *spiritual* journey: a quest to discover my own beliefs, my own deepest needs and who I truly am.

I deliberately use the term spiritual rather than religious because, whilst both hold the potential for transcendent experiences and experiences of God, the Beloved, the Divine (there are many terms for that which is pretty much indescribable but 'the Divine', for me, holds the concept of that power, that presence, which is the essence of all life, of all things, of the whole universe), there is a fundamental difference that proved to be very important to me.

神
God
Supernatural
power

My roots were in the Christian faith and my spiritual journey evolved out of this more religious part into an increasingly self-directed and self-determining path. I feel that followers in the major faiths are led (if not actually told) to what they *should* believe and, often, how they *should* follow those beliefs. This is frequently a control issue, with the 'powers that be' often holding considerable power over the members of their community. If people were allowed to think for themselves and, even more radical perhaps, if individuals were encouraged to trust their own experiences and to validate those experiences, it is likely that those in power would lose a great deal of their control.

Religions usually have particular frameworks, with fairly clear tenets of belief, and the authority of others which the individual has to accept, especially if they wish to go through the membership rite of the particular faith group or community. In contrast, the spiritual path is about personal responsibility, self-determination, openness to whatever experiences may come my way, a sense of creating my own path, discovering what *I* believe and what my 'raison d'être' might be.

My Awakening

My awakening to the possibilities of a journey of a very different nature from anything I had previously considered was not an overnight phenomenon. I often wondered if I was simply a slow learner yet, in hindsight, I realise that the vague sense of unease, of searching for something, was not enough of a spur for me to take any radical actions. A traumatic experience (the death of Neil, my husband, in 1991) was the catalyst, in the end, that led to profound changes and a completely different direction for my life. It was only after this that I could see the preparation that had already taken place in my spiritual awareness. There is also something about needing the experiences I had already had before I was ready or able to accept and incorporate the shifts in my understanding and my beliefs.

> "Most of us do not consciously choose our initiation. It appears just to happen, and often is quite a shock."
>
> **Carol Pearson,** *Awakening the Heroes Within,* p42. HarperSanFrancisco, 1991.

In 1994, at the request of Bryce Taylor, I wrote the following account of my awakening as an example of complex grief for his book *Helping People Change*.

> In 1985 Neil and I were invited to be godparents to a friend's newborn daughter and during the christening service in the local Anglican Church I was hit by the certainty that there was something missing in my life. It was a very strong feeling at the time which then became buried underneath the ensuing celebrations, return to work and 'normal' life. Then in 1987 I attended the ordination service of that same friend in Ripon Cathedral. It was the first time for many years that I had been to a full church service and it was my first experience of an ordination service. At one point in that service there was something called the Peace. This was a new (and alien) experience for me and involved people turning to those around them 'to exchange a sign of peace' – usually a handshake. As I happened to be sitting at the end of a pew one of the clergy involved in the service – one with a very striking cloak (which I now know is a cope) that had amazing coloured flames running up it – shook my hand.

I was shaken to the core. At the moment of contact with this unknown person, I experienced what felt like an electric current flowing through his hand into mine, up my arm and through my body. I looked into his eyes – not something I would normally do – and there was what I would now call mutual recognition; a meeting of souls. At that time I did not know what to think, I did not know what had happened, I did not know who he was or what any consequences might be. All I did know was this could not be ignored. So I turned to the only place I knew – the Christian church. I was confirmed later that year and started training as a Reader[2] the following year, but even that did not take away the sense that there was more, though I still had no sense what the 'more' was. Soon, however, all of this went completely out of my head.

My husband's sudden death in 1991 at the age of 41 turned everything upside down and took me on a path I never even knew was possible or existed. It is a path which has led me through many desperate, dark, fear and tear-filled days. It has led me to many insights, new awakenings – wonderful, magical moments alongside hard-hitting and sobering truths which are difficult to accept. This journey is still continuing, and always will.

[2] My training to be licensed as a Reader in the Church of England took the form of a two year part-time course covering theology, the roles and responsibilities of the Reader, the practicalities of delivering sermons, leading services as well as practical experience in my parishes under the supervision of my parish priest. Once I was licensed, in addition to preaching two or three times each month, my particular commitments included pastoral care (primarily in bereavement situations), working with children and young people, and leading study groups.

Four months after his death, even I could tell I wasn't coping and I broke down in tears in the staff room at school. School sent me home via my GP who, in turn, sent me to a Community Psychiatric Nurse (CPN) who began the very painstaking process of breaking through my barriers. I will be forever grateful to him – though I certainly wasn't at the time – for his patience and his directness, and his lack of avoidance of difficult subjects. Towards the end of the time we spent together, he recommended I attend a six month counselling skills course. It was whilst I was on this course that I was fortunate enough to be found by someone (B[3]) who was willing to travel with me through whatever this journey brought my way.

He was the guest facilitator halfway through the counselling course and part of his input concerned trauma and the signs of someone who was traumatised. Inwardly, I was ticking off all the signs and symptoms and it was quite a shock to realise and recognise that I was, by these criteria, traumatised and that, perhaps, I was not managing my grief in a particularly healthy or useful way. In the lunch break I asked a rather fatuous question, 'Did you mean all that?' Well, of course he did! And it wasn't the real question, but I didn't know what that was. In the event, he offered me help which I, eventually, accepted. He later told me that he could 'see' something in me and, in that sense, he was drawn to work with me. Many years later when I asked what

[3] 'B' refers to Bryce Taylor who was my counsellor at the time (see *Chapter 8 Healing Through Meeting* for a description of how this relationship developed and the critical role it has played in my life). In his book we followed the convention of using his initial rather than his full name and I have retained that here.

it was he could 'see' he talked of recognising a spiritual dimension within me; one that I was using to inform how I moved forward. This was my first experience of that idea of 'knowing' something that was other than a form of academic or intellectual knowledge.

I had a powerful resistance to revealing feelings, even to owning their very existence. I had a seemingly ever-increasing need to cry yet I knew this to be wrong. Crying is a weakness, a loss of self-control. 'What on earth will others think if I cry, after all it's 12, 18 months, two years ago since IT happened.' Only people who can't cope cry and I can cope with anything – I've believed this always, so it must be true! And anyway, 'good' Christians don't need to cry because they should be able to use their faith to sustain them and gain serenity.

I didn't know how to 'let go'. Self-control was my prime directive. I did not know how to allow my feelings to just be. I did not know how to accept them, work with them and so move on. Fear of rejection was huge. Fear of being laughed at was equally huge.

Over many sessions, I began to see that B was in a totally different place from me. Tears were not a threat to him. They were not even signs of weakness. They were not to be avoided or scorned. He was not judging me. All the judgements, all the 'shoulds' and 'oughts' were from me. 'I should have more control.' 'I should not need to cry.' 'I ought to be able to think all this through logically.' He began to tell me when I was judgemental. I never realised how often I would put myself down or castigate myself for the way I was feeling at any given moment.

This continued for many years (I remain awake to this trait), and I gradually began to be aware of what I said and, more to the point, how I seemed to judge everything black or white. And it was becoming apparent that I had one rule for me and another one for everyone else. It is OK for others to cry. It is OK for others to show anger etc – but not for me. I should be able to control these feelings.

I was beginning to see a new way. This way means honesty. Honesty with myself as to how I am feeling. This way means accepting how I feel, allowing it to be, allowing my feelings to teach me the way forward. I began to allow my feelings to show yet I was still very fearful that I might be completely consumed by their power. I had come to realise that the sadness and the tears were only part of the fear of feelings. There were other, even less acceptable feelings lurking under the surface. Anger, hatred, and jealousy were all there waiting to consume me. I was frightened – no, I was terrified – of allowing these free reign. The power they had. The strength of feeling I had never, never experienced before. How could I control them? How could I keep pushing them down and pretend they didn't exist. The answer to both, of course, was that if I wanted to learn anything, if I simply wanted to survive, then I couldn't.

I remember little of this time. It was an enormous effort to get up, to wash and dress. I fell into a

Pit from which there seemed no escape. It was a bottomless, dark, dank place. My days consisted simply of existing – and what was the point of such an existence? I had no great desire to go on living. I had no desire for anything. I had no interest in anything. Life felt dead; I might as well be – so the thoughts ran. The motorway bridge gained a kind of morbid fascination and what stopped me was the belief that I wouldn't even get that right – I'd only be badly injured instead of dead.

The fear, the despair, the loneliness, the strength of feelings seemed to possess me totally day in and day out. There was a feeling of having lost everything. A feeling of total emptiness and blackness.

Many of those feelings, parts of the real me, were, I believed, really not acceptable. They are negative. They are definitely not Christian and certainly 'nice' people don't have them. I began to learn of my shadow side. Over time I began to accept it as part of being human, truly human and alive.

There was so much fear. Fear, again, of what would happen if I really lost control and said EXACTLY what I wanted to. Fear of rejection.

Through many discussions concerning the early implanting of messages and through reading books on sexual issues and life scripts, I also began to realise how repressed and suppressed I had been and still was as an adult. It is only since that stage that I am now able to work more on what it means to be a woman – to be female as against the asexual being I had learned to be.

Previously, I had compartmentalised everything – physical energy, nervous energy, emotional energy and sexual energy. I now realise they are all part of one whole. I was denying myself access to a tremendous source of energy. This meant that I was not living fully and that I limited the possibilities for my growth.

I would stay with one issue long after I had really worked through it because it felt safe. Even if it was hellish – at least I knew the issue, I knew where I was. I can still catch myself doing this – hanging on to things long past my need for them or their usefulness to me; an avoidance of moving on. Letting go of one thing inevitably meant dealing with something else. And there seemed to be so much. My whole world had disintegrated and there did not seem to be a single element of my life that was comfortable or stable or familiar.

I had no husband; I didn't have an identity anymore; many illusions of my childhood had disintegrated; illusions concerning my marriage had gone: all my foundations were under severe threat. So much change, so much lost. Letting go took courage and a lot of support and energy.

Throughout the whole of this time, I had relied very heavily on the faith I had as a Christian. Even at my darkest time – in the Pit – I did not feel deserted by God. At least I still had that. The strong, tangible presence of God the first night after my husband's death remains with me still. At times, I felt as though He was literally holding my hand. It was a very physical experience as well as a spiritual one. Yet, in other ways my beliefs were a handicap to me; many were inherited from childhood and they had a straitjacket effect on the way I viewed things.

As part of the work with me, B suggested I receive massage. I can now recognise that my body held so much and it was key to helping me let go and become a feeling person instead of a robot existing from day to day. During the bodywork, I had some experiences that I found frightening and weird. It was the beginning of wondering whether I was going mad.

During one memorable session, I found myself amongst dolphins. It was as if I was at one with them because I did not need to come up for air in the way I would do if I was just swimming with dolphins. I felt the freedom in the ocean; I heard the conversations between us; I was welcomed and accepted by them. It was this acceptance and welcome that was particularly stunning to me – after all, I was not accepted by myself so how come they could accept me?

At first, I was very reluctant to talk about the experience since I genuinely wondered if I was going mad, and, even more, expected Maggie (the person giving me the massages) to think I was going mad. When I began to have more such strange and different experiences in other sessions B encouraged me to tell her. I did; she wasn't at all surprised. It was good to be able to share them and to have my experiences accepted as perfectly normal.

Then, in one session she said it was time for me to put my hands on her. Well, I'd never heard anything so ridiculous! Anyway, she lay down and suggested I just let my hands touch where it felt right. I had no idea how but my hands did know where to go – where healing was needed. There was an incredible heat in my hands too, to which she drew my attention and even though I tried to pass it off as heat because I was working I knew deep down it was not an ordinary temperature kind of heat. There was an intuitive sense of 'knowing'.

I found the experiences, the insights into healing, the growing awareness of other ways of being, other ways of operating that I was gaining through massage and through energy work strange but exhilarating. I was experiencing things I never knew existed. I was finding I was far less judgemental, after all I didn't know what was going to happen next. As I left one session B asked me to hold out my hand; in it he placed a stone and asked me what I could feel. It was really weird – I could feel heat and a kind of tingling yet it was 'only' a stone. It was my first experience of what I might now call subtle energy.

This process so far had taken something over 15 months. Then, something happened which altered everything. A comment was made in a session about the veracity of parts of the Bible, and I was thrown into utter despair. I lost everything. I had no God. The one thing which had sustained me, the thing I felt had kept me from committing suicide, the one lifeline through the Pit, through the months of pain and agony. That was gone. I felt destroyed. Why that? Now, I had absolutely nothing left. WHY had He deserted me? I know what it is like to feel to be in Hell.

I think I can now understand something of the desperation leading to suicide. It was only the many conversations with my priest and the hours spent by B talking me through it that enabled me to survive intact. 'This is your "crucifixion" and after that is the resurrection. You had faith in your faith.' This I did not understand, but now is becoming much clearer and is accurate. I now see this sequence of events as instrumental: I had to discover for myself 'the desert'; I had to give up faith and trust *experience* – my experience. He also talked of taking 'Christ out of Christianity'; a phrase which gradually grew in meaning and importance for me.

A change began about a week later. I was early for a bodywork session and I went into the site of a ruined Abbey. I'd had no plans for that and I still don't know how the trip was so quick as to give me the time to do so. There was an irresistible urge to kneel there on the stone floor. The sun shone through onto me. One question I asked, 'What more do you want from me?' The answer was clear but said in love, 'Everything. Then I can begin to fill you'. I now realised that anything I put between myself and God would be taken away. Not long ago I would have said this kind of experience didn't happen to people like me. This was happening to me, not some erudite theologian or academic or some 'way-out' sixties hippie or high flying 'New Age' guru!

This was the turning point. I KNEW that I had not been permanently deserted. The desert (as I came to think of it) was instrumental in heralding the next and most exciting stage so far in my journey. All my foundations, all my values and beliefs were under threat – but I knew God was there.

In June of that year I was at the top of Red Pike in the Lake District with a group of A Level Geography students. We were enveloped by thick, freezing mist, unable to see very much at all, when I suddenly became aware of God. I could hear sheep, birds, a stream, feel the dampness, hear muted conversations and I knew that God was still creating in all this, as well as in me. I began to feel such warmth – not physical because it was very cold, but inside – a warmth. Such a strong awareness; awareness that He wants me to come closer to Him; to learn more about Him. It was a fantastic feeling of being surrounded by God; like another anorak – a layer surrounding all of me.

Some time previously, B had said he was looking forward to seeing me drown. At the time I was irritated (really angry, actually, but I couldn't own such a 'negative' feeling at that time). I already felt as though I was drowning; that I was barely able to keep my head above water; that it might actually be better if I did drown. And now, here I was, on top of a mountain feeling as though I was drowning in His love. An awesome experience.

Then, in August 1993, I had a magical three weeks.

At the beginning of the month, I visited Rievaulx Abbey (a place that has become very precious to me) for the first time. As I entered the grounds I felt such a sense of history: of connection with all that has ever been at the Abbey, all that is at the Abbey and all that will be there at any time in the future. I experienced an overwhelming sense of peace and of belonging. Tears rolled down my cheeks; tears of joy, wonderment, thanksgiving, and of fear, too, in that the feeling might not last. And of course it couldn't. Yet I also knew that it was not lost; it was there to be experienced again and it was there for me to feel that I belonged – a novel experience for me. The feelings stayed with me very powerfully for about three weeks and then became a little less euphoric in their intensity.

Another significant event at this time involved healing. I was having a lot of pain in my jaw – the result of a dislocation from a sporting injury about 18 months previously that had not responded at all to conventional approaches. I became aware of the strong connection between the lingering pain and the concept of holding on: holding onto my emotions; holding onto my belief system; holding onto my old behaviour patterns. As B worked on my jaw to relieve the pain it also released emotional pain. Each time this happened I felt tremendous relief and the sense of no longer needing to hold everything inside me. So, more tears. And I wasn't giving myself such a hard time about that anymore either.

During this time I also gained insights about Jesus; his role, who he is/was; he was neither Victim nor Rescuer (to use TA[4] language) but he was a Liberator. He was on earth to show a way to freedom; a way to live who we truly are.

Additionally in this three-week period, I had the understanding that:

---

[4] TA (Transactional Analysis) is a model for understanding human personality, relationships and communication. It was first developed by the late Eric Berne, MD. See the following books for further information: *Games People Play: The Psychology of Human Relationships*, Eric Berne, Penguin Books, London; *I'm OK, You're OK*, Thomas A Harris, Pan Books; *T A Today: A New Introduction to Transactional Analysis,* Ian Stewart & Vann Joines, Lifespace Publishing, England.

> It is not where I am; it is not what I do; it is not what I say: it is my intent, my approach, my attitude that holds the key.

It felt fairly obvious afterwards yet it was the beginning of being able to make a fundamental shift in my approach to how I live my life.

As the different strands of my journey continue to weave in and out of each other they feel as they are becoming more at one. With less separation between them, it feels as though I am becoming more at one – with myself and with God. There are many marvellous times when the penny drops – when realisation dawns – often about something I've struggled with for ages; something which B has been telling me about for ages.

Yet there are still times when I feel lost. Times when I feel distraught. Times when I feel I have to speak to someone – hear a friendly voice or go insane.

I have great difficulty at times accepting all this. Is this really me? Is this a permanent transformation or a temporary high spot which will go when I'm no longer in the environment where this kind of spiritual journey is actively sought after and encouraged?

I KNOW I can fly – but my wings feel very small and inexperienced. I wish, more than anything else I can think of, to continue this journey. I wish to learn so much more about the concepts and issues I have touched on in the last two years. A journey which I

> now know was essential for me to begin to develop into a whole, feeling human being, but one which has not been easy and could not have been done alone.

Although this was written over 15 years ago, it is still important and relevant for me and it was the gateway into discovering other ways of being. I gradually began to accept that this reality – the socially accepted norm – is not all that there is; it is but one of many realities. I have always believed that there were things beyond our understanding, but now I was experiencing them. I believe this is available to all of us in our own way, with our own particular styles, gifts and experiences.

During my awakening I began to experience totally unexpected images, visions, feelings, activities that took me into realms I did not know even existed. The dolphins were only the beginning! Having someone to talk to about these was crucial – and still is. Many, many times I really wondered if I was going mad. Were these experiences my imagination? Were these experiences an indication that I was schizophrenic or something similar? Were these experiences simply the manifestation of wishful thinking or an avoidance of 'real life'?

For example, in 1994 I visited Kirkstall Abbey in Leeds on my way to a massage session and, unusually, the main gates were unlocked and open. It was difficult to go in. There was a strong and clear sense that once I stepped through those open gates I would be entering a new and different world. I knew that once I walked through there would be no turning back. 'People' down the sides of the Abbey church were smiling and encouraging me to enter; to join them and leave my old world behind. As I took that fateful step there was an overwhelming sense of welcoming, of belonging. I felt myself to be, I was, part of everything around me – the Abbey, the trees, the blue sky, the sounds of the river close by, history, all those beings down the side of the Abbey. As I walked down the church I felt as though I'd grown, physically as well as metaphorically.

Later that same month I suddenly found myself flying with a kestrel I had been watching. I could see the world through his eyes. I could feel the energy it took to spread his wings, hover and then dive to seize his prey. It was an amazing view – a bird's eye view and a very different perspective.

Not long after this experience I was sitting on the moors in the Yorkshire Dales reading *Spiritual Healing* by Jack Angelo and, once again, I felt myself to be part of everything around me; rocks, bilberries, heather, sky, sun – everything. There was no demarcation, no edges and yet no element lost its own unique identity either. Then I was suffused by an overwhelming knowing that at the centre of all this, of all things, is love. Love which comes from understanding, from compassion, from un-attachment, from acceptance of myself and all others as spiritual beings.

A couple of months later I was on a residential course when, one morning, I felt so full of energy (not physical energy but a buzzing kind of energy I came to know as subtle energy) that I just did not know what to do with it. It was my first experience of such levels of energy and I had no means of either managing it or utilising it. I mentioned this in the opening round and one of the facilitators suggested I get up and walk around the group to give healing to whoever needed it.

At first I had all the familiar messages in my head: I can't do that; I don't know how to do that. But, once I was standing and able to push those thoughts further back I just knew! I knew who was in most need and I knew where in their bodies the healing was needed, or what the issue was that was causing them pain. I would have been incredibly sceptical if I had been told about this but here I was experiencing it for myself. I even had the opportunity of receiving feedback from those involved, which indicated that I was absolutely spot on, so there was no way I could kid myself that it was my imagination or I'd made it up or I was going mad or it was a dream or they were just 'being kind'. It also helped to have the facilitator normalising this – as though it was the most natural thing in the world rather than something of which to be frightened, to shy away from or believe is an indication of impending madness.

The final part of this particular experience was the most challenging for me. The facilitator asked me to give the healing energy to the most important person in the room that needed it. I was a bit lost at this. I looked around but I felt that I'd done what needed to be done with the others in the group. He persisted and persisted until, finally, I grasped it. He meant me. It wasn't that I didn't think I needed healing, I knew I did – and do – it was more the concept of my being the 'most important'. That was alien to me so hearing it like that and feeling its genuineness was a huge challenge to my then world-view.

The spontaneous nature of those first experiences actually gave them a validity all of their own. I could not, in my wildest dreams, have imagined some of the events that took place, such as the realignment of my jaw following dislocation even when all I had hoped for was a reduction in the pain levels. There was no physical contact, just his hands a few inches away from both sides of my face. On the drive home things felt different and then the following day I realised that my jaw was almost back to its healthy position. It took further sessions before the change became permanent but the influence of this has been far wider than the physical outcome.

I was being challenged to look at things differently. After all, how could this happen? There had been no form of physical manipulation. There had been no contact at all and yet I had – and still have – the evidence of something 'impossible' happening.

This was to become a theme of my journey – especially in the earlier years. The impossible was suddenly no longer always impossible. My once rigid views of the laws of the universe and what is and is not possible were pulled up short. If 'this' were possible – and I had my own experience to back it up – what else would be possible? I was challenged to drop many of the structures I had been told were true and many of the things I had been told to believe, both in a religious sense and in a more general context of understanding how the universe works. In my journey to who I truly am, the fundamental challenge was developing trust in my own experience.

The events and experiences described above formed the building bricks from which I created and developed a whole new life and way of being. It was an agonising time yet it was also a glorious time of rebirth and, in hindsight, I wouldn't wish it to have been any different. I now know what it is like to live but not be alive. I now **feel**; I now am aware of so much more; I see things differently; I hold myself differently; I am alive.

2

Travelling into the Shadowlands

"Our greatest glory is not in never falling, but in rising every time we fall." **Confucius**

Introduction

I had begun to see that another way of being was possible and that another world was beckoning. This meant that I had to focus on those beliefs, patterns and behaviours that operated in my day-to-day life in less than useful and healthy ways. I discovered very early on that I did not have the spaciousness, the energy, or even the will to deal with bigger issues such as spiritual matters without first clearing some of my personal 'baggage'. I knew I must be willing to face my shortcomings, my personal 'demons' and my own 'shadow' side before I was able to countenance operating differently in interpersonal arenas, which, in turn, would enable me to enter the realms of the transpersonal[5] more fully, more clearly and more completely.

[5] The term transpersonal is usually used to refer to psychological categories that transcend the normal features of ordinary ego-functioning: events move beyond the rational and precede the mystical. The term is often associated with the work of Abraham Maslow and his understanding of 'peak experiences'.

"When a man seeks obstacles to measure his strength he goes towards the *north*.

If he needs rest and tranquillity he turns to the *south*

To learn of his future he sets off to the *west*

And he returns to the *east* to discover his origins

But for the longest of voyages he travels motionless, *inside* himself."

Uman

As I grew up, I absorbed the mores of my surroundings, including home, school and the wider community, without even realising it. I learned about my place in the world, my sense of whether I was 'somebody', whether I needed to be like this or that in order to be good or acceptable or loveable. All of these influenced how I saw myself in relation to others and thus had a direct impact upon how I lived. There was so much of my life and the way I operated that was outside my conscious awareness which meant that, more often than not, I did not get the responses I craved. I couldn't understand why and I didn't know how to be different in order to get what I did want. This time of facing my darker side is what I call the *Shadowlands*.

"Recovery lies in the places we avoid." **Arthur Miller**

This chapter therefore looks at the fundamental issues that were holding me where I was: working with my shadow; facing my terror; transcending my ego; learning about the 'deficit economy'; discovering my safe place; claiming my power; working with pain; having to stop and what this meant in my life; learning much more about the human condition and I how relate to others.

The Shadow

> "The shadow is the part that no one talks about, although it is usually the most significant issue in personal as well as in group life."
>
> **Bryce Taylor**, *Forging the Future Together,* p84. Oasis Press, 2003.

The shadow relates to those aspects of myself that influence how I behave, what I do, choices I make and so on, but which are often not yet conscious. If my assumptions about the world, myself, how others see me and how I perceive others see me are left hidden and unexplored then my behaviour becomes more and more driven, and less and less helpful to my development and process. Transactional Analysis (TA) describes some of these behaviours through the concept of five 'Drivers'.

Figure 1: The Five Drivers

I was affected by all five drivers to a lesser or greater degree and on occasions still find myself particularly challenged by 'be perfect'. My belief goes that I need to be perfect, never to get things wrong, in order to be accepted and loved by others. It has been very hard, and involved what felt to be considerable risk-taking, for me to move beyond this and to believe that 'good enough' is actually all that is necessary at times. And, perhaps more importantly, that there are people – many people – who do not in any way link their acceptance and love of me with my always getting things right and being good at things.

In certain situations, mainly in groups, I had a way of behaving that was almost a form of autopilot; patterns I fell into because they had been with me for so long. I couldn't, for example, understand why others saw me as being manipulative and needy in groups. It took a long, long process of looking at the mechanisms of how the patterns lived in me before I was able to recognise how they operated – unconsciously – and how I could do things differently to gain the responses I was craving, i.e. acceptance and a sense of belonging.

Working with my shadow also meant being willing to face my demons – those things I feared others discovering about me – and developing the belief that I do have a place in the world and that I have the right to exist. As a consequence of working in this way, I began to gain a more balanced and realistic perception of my place with other people as well as gaining a clearer and straighter relationship with myself.

This process of bringing the shadow into the light required time, a commitment to myself and, more often than not, finding safe places and people with whom to explore the whole idea. It was essential, if painful at times.

> Freedom is the degree to which we have intimacy with our shadow side.

Being free in this context does not then mean that I tell everybody everything about me – we all have personal areas that will remain personal and private. The key is having the freedom to choose: freedom to disclose or not; freedom to speak out or not; freedom to be at a particular event or not. When this position is reached, I no longer have a *pathological* need to hide something, to avoid an issue, say, or certain people but, instead, I can make free and aware choices that enable me to be fully present to whatever degree is appropriate for a particular situation.

Transcending the Ego

The analogy of the onion (stripping away layers one by one) is a familiar one in personal development and counselling, and it is a good one – as far as it goes. Certainly, as I learn about myself or gain new insight into how I am perceived by others, there is always something else waiting to be learned, acknowledged, discovered. Some of the issues I have faced are life-long ones that return in different guises; however, as I learn more about them, they become less of an issue for me and therefore they have less control of and power over me.

But there is a major flaw in the analogy of the onion: the idea is not to get rid of, for example, some belief or some behaviour pattern but rather to come to understand more of what it is about; to integrate it into who I am in order to transform those parts that are distorted and which get in my way of relating to others and/or the universe.

It was at this point that I began to grasp more clearly the idea that light and dark co-exist; one cannot exist without the other. I also learned that as I spent more time in the 'light', the periods when I fell back into the dark seemed more dark, more desperate, more all-encompassing than before – quite simply the contrast between the times I was in my power, when I was centred and when I was operating from a more authentic place brought the darker times into stark relief and contrast.

It was a salutary moment when I realised that I was not the person I thought I was: that I was not, after all, completely 'nice'; that some of my motives were far less altruistic than I wanted to believe. Harder still was accepting that this was OK; that having my shadow, my failings, my mistakes did not make me a 'bad' person. Beauty and the Beast are both within me and are a natural part of the human condition: the light and dark co-existing.

Beauty and the Beast

Beauty and the Beast are one and the same
There is the beast in all of us
There is beauty in all of us
One does not exist without the other
There is passion in the beast
Gentleness/compassion in the beauty
To divide them is to destroy
To attempt to eliminate the beast is to create a shallow, pale imitation of life
To intertwine, to integrate, to transform, to balance
In this lies the work
In this lies humanity and divinity irrevocably intertwined

Heather Tweddle

Learning to accept my failures and all the ways I fall into patterned behaviour is important, but this is not the same as 'anything goes' or excusing everything by claiming 'this is the way I am' as though a certain behaviour is set in concrete and unchangeable. Neither is it the same as saying that I do not seek to develop my responses and my ways of relating to others. This is more about a continuing process of looking at my behaviours, especially my shadow side, in order to learn more about myself and to have more choices about how I behave and to have more effective, straight ways to gain the responses I need. This way leads to growth and development rather than setting myself up to fail when the pattern returns or I find myself behaving or responding in *that* way again.

This is nothing more – and nothing less – than endeavouring to *transcend the ego*. As I explore my shadow side, as I grow in freedom, as I create greater spaciousness within, as I am able to move beyond my driven patterns and behaviours so I am able to let go of my ego-driven needs and concerns in what I say, do or claim. There is no place for the ego that seeks personal gratification or fame or glory. A personal agenda can get in the way of openness to the Divine; can get in the way of meeting with the Divine; can get in the way of discovering my truest, sacred Self.

Facing my Terror

Facing the anxiety, fear and then the terror I constantly felt had to be addressed very early on. These states literally controlled my life. I had no freedom in how to respond in so many situations. I lived on what I came to call 'red alert'; always looking for the attack that could come from anywhere and anyone. It was all-consuming and incredibly demanding of energy. By choice, for example, I would always sit with my back to a wall in cafes and other public spaces so that I could see what was happening and could not be surprised by anything or anyone coming from behind.

I think I had known – albeit unconsciously – even as a child and teenager that I lived with anxiety. I remember at the age of eight or nine sitting at the top of the stairs outside my bedroom long after I was supposed to be in bed asleep listening to see if I could hear my parents' voices. This was to make sure they were both still there and that I had not been deserted. There is absolutely no rational basis for that fear in my life; I never even heard them ever argue let alone any talk or threat of leaving.

In addition, from childhood, into teenage years and then to college, I felt huge anxiety around the whole friendship thing. I was never sure any first move towards someone would be welcome; something I now recognise as part of my lack of confidence and sense of not belonging. However, it was not until June 1993, when my right foot was being massaged, that I experienced such absolute fear that I was overwhelmed. I felt that I was being held down. I wanted to break free; 'leave me alone', screamed inside my head.

It was two years later that something happened to catapult me into such a place of terror that I, literally, lost control of myself and did not even know what I was doing. As part of a two-year course in Energetic Integration we were looking at birth, early childhood, formation of patterns, life experiences of babies and young children, and how all this can be held in the body and affect us later in life. One person, as part of the practical work, cried (screamed) like a baby and I went to a place of such absolute terror that I ran out of the building bare-footed, across a main road and just fell onto a grass verge.

I had no awareness other than terror. I had no consciousness other than terror. I had no sense of me other than through the terror.

When I was brought back into the room I could barely speak, was barely able to function and needed to sit quietly wrapped in blankets for some considerable time. Even then, I was unable to give a coherent account of what had happened. All I really knew was what I felt and I felt as though I was lost in a terrifying world beyond my knowledge and understanding.

In the following months it became clear that the terror was held in my body and I now know much of it also stemmed from memories from past life experiences. A few months later, someone greeted me with a friendly touch on the back of my neck. I screamed and my blood seemed to freeze. For a long time after that first experience, even the slightest touch on the back of my neck had the same response. I felt I was being held; something around my neck. I knew 'they' were coming to 'get me'. They were going to capture me. No matter what I said or did to avoid them, it was never enough. They would always find me. They would capture me; they intended to kill me.

Over a long period, being able to work on this with someone who was unafraid of such deep and strong emotions was my lifeline. In many of the sessions I experienced a very real sense of release – once I was able to allow myself to go into whatever arose. The fear of what I might find, what I might feel, of being totally and utterly consumed by the terror was so real. This fear simply deepened the terror and made it an even more daunting prospect.

Gradually, I began to have memories; memories that had been held deep in my body. I remembered major surgery I'd had on my neck when I was 19; surgery that I'd always ignored as though it had never happened. And yet it was a serious 'attack' on my spine, on my body, with a number of follow-up procedures needed as well. I remembered being hunted as a child in a past life experience. I experienced the horror of being burned at the stake as a witch.

Alongside the pain and horror of experiences of this nature, came greater insight, learning and understanding into how I was feeling and what I was holding in my body.

It became apparent that the terror was not simply mine; it was (is) mine to work with but it is much greater than me too. I was connecting with and tapping into the collective unconscious[6]. Work on my neck led to much screaming, yet as I worked on it in a safe place, allowing the terror its voice and listening to my body to hear what it needed me to know, experience or acknowledge, I slowly began to be more free of it in my day-to-day life. As part of that process I 'wrote' to the Terror.

The Terror

The Terror is part of me – yet it belongs to the past
The Terror is a guide to more truth – if I allow it to be
The Terror is real yet not real; it is now yet not now
The Terror will never leave me completely yet I know it will change; it will be different when I am able to communicate with it – when I can learn to accept it and not fight it

So, no longer an aim of getting rid of or fighting the terror, but coming together with it; allowing it to be; getting to know it

Then it will be different
Then it will be a guide, an ally, my teacher

Heather Tweddle

---

6 The unconscious part of our mind is the possessor of extraordinary knowledge; it knows more than we know as our conscious self. When we become aware of a new truth, it is because we recognise it to be true; we re-know that which we knew all along.

During some of the healing sessions, I 'saw' black threads emanating from the back of my neck; I felt a malignant presence, wanting to kill me by attacking my neck; I felt the tightness of a noose and the horror of a sword stroke across the back of my neck. All these led to shaking in my body; shaking that had to be felt and allowed to pass through.

It was a long and challenging process – for both of us, I think – but I know it was absolutely vital. It took courage and determination. The 'demons' had to be acknowledged and worked with. My body needed to be heard; it needed to be nurtured; it needed recognition for all that it had enabled me to do – in spite of surgery and injuries. Eventually I experienced a sense of greater inner peace and space, and there was less fear. I had lived at least on 'yellow alert' for most of my life and on 'red alert' since entering this phase; it was so different to be no longer constantly on the look out for the next attack.

The defining moment for me was when I felt the terror flood down and out of my body to be replaced by joy; sheer unadulterated, free joy. This was not a familiar feeling – in fact I don't think I have felt such joy flood through my body as on that particular moment. It was the instant I also realised that here was the final piece of the jigsaw in this phase. This occurred on February 1st 2000, 7 years after my descent into the terror. I know, too, that everything else had to be done first for there to be the space for the joy; for there to be the inner freedom to experience such a contrast in emotion. It is a day I will never forget.

No Home to Call my Own

In addition to feeling terror and being constantly on the alert for danger from somewhere, anywhere, I believed that I didn't *belong* anywhere. Belonging is often about feeling safe, having somewhere to be part of what is going on and, importantly, being seen to be a part, yet I did not feel safe anywhere and I felt that I belonged nowhere. There was no place I went as part of my daily life where I felt at ease or acceptable.

Gradually I came to see that I felt this way because I did not belong to myself. The place of safety I needed to find was not out in the world but within me; a place that would go with me wherever life's course would lead me and into whatever events and experiences came my way.

Really knowing that I had a place in the world, that I was acceptable in the world and that I did have a right to be alive was one of the most remarkable shifts in my view of myself and my relationship to the world. Belonging then became a very different issue altogether. I learned that belonging to a particular group or team, say, became a matter of choice and that it is part of my taking on greater personal responsibility for how I act or respond in any and every situation.

Gradually, it dawned on me that I belong to the universe. I have had many experiences of being connected to all things and one of the first was incredibly powerful because I felt not only *connected* with all that is, was and will be but also that I *belonged* with all that too.

An event that really brought this home to me was during a visit to Bryce Canyon in the US. As I looked across the magical rock formations with their amazing colours and mystical feel, I became aware of history; so much history. I could 'see' an old – yet not old – man, a Native American Indian, standing on top of one of the pillars. I experienced a deep, profound sense of stillness, of quiet, of peace yet considerable bewilderment too.

Other people and animals were there. There was a coyote on top of a pillar. It lived there, part of the rock; living with and part of the landscape, always there. The landscape is alive; it has a spirit of its own; living in **balance** with the seasons. I knew then that Humanity can live in harmony with the landscape but we have lost so much; we have given so much away; we have forgotten so much in the drive for technology and more, more of everything. Both the Man and the Coyote were – are – Guardians of the land. They guard the silence, the wonder, the connectedness, the Balance.

It was so clear that I was being welcomed into this. I was being given such a gift; a gift of being able to see, hear, feel, experience, live so much more than is usual. But even more than all of that, I was given the gift of recognition; I was given the gift of invitation;

I was given the gift of acceptance; I was given the gift of belonging. I also began to grasp the edge of something that has since grown: the understanding that this has always been here for me. **I was part of all this;** always have been, always will be. It was only now that I had the awareness, the spaciousness, the openness to enter into this space and reality. Perhaps the most powerful legacy of all from this experience is the knowledge that no-one can destroy my **soul**, my **being**, the real **'I'**.

Physical Breakdown

Although I generally had what some would call 'low self-esteem' for as long as I can remember, there was one area of my life in which I had confidence and some pride. This was my physical capabilities in sports of varying kinds. I was fit; I was good at team sports; I was agile; I had excellent balance in gymnastics; I was always wanted pretty much first for teams; I was school House Sports Captain. So no-one was surprised that my chosen career was to become a specialist PE teacher in secondary schools as well as, for some years, an instructor at an Outdoor Activities Centre.

My interest in sports continued. I met my husband on the Judo mat; I progressed rapidly through Judo gradings and became a member of the Scottish Judo squad, having won a bronze medal at the Scottish Open Championships. I played league hockey every winter weekend and ran either six or ten miles every day. All this whilst teaching PE full-time.

This trend continued for many years until, in 1997, I received a serious hockey injury that needed long-term outpatient hospital treatment. Most of my upper teeth were broken and needed to be taken out, but this could not be done for almost four months in order to give time for the surrounding bone to heal or I would be disfigured. The pain at this time was overwhelming and eating confined to bananas, soup and soft foods.

I had to stop playing hockey; in fact I had to stop all sporting activities. It was only then that I recognised how much I had forced myself to play in the hockey match, compete on the judo mat, go running, because 'I will be fine when I get there'. And, indeed, most of the time I was, and the friendships, the companionship and the satisfaction of doing something well overruled the effort it took.

For many years I had sustained a considerable number of injuries and I simply played through them – as many sports people do – and continued being involved in physically demanding, strongly competitive sports, ignoring any messages my body was giving me that it had, actually, had enough. But I now had to stop everything and I discovered how exhausted I was.

The levels of pain throughout my body were almost unbearable and pretty much constant. Getting up in the morning was a huge act of will. Having showered and had breakfast I could only summon energy to go back to bed. It was tough. I felt distraught – the one area in my life in which I had always had confidence had been taken away from me.

By this time I had left full-time teaching and was working as a self-employed massage therapist and counsellor, but I began to realise that even this could not continue. My wrists were so painful I couldn't even carry shopping let alone massage anyone. Every joint in my body hurt; every movement became an act of will. I went to see my GP knowing I could not carry on as I was and I was concerned there might be a serious underlying problem. I received a diagnosis of Chronic Fatigue Syndrome (CFS) (or ME, depending on the practitioner).

The specialist to whom I was referred gave two solutions – exercise, which I was desperate to do at all costs but couldn't, and anti-depressants, which I really did not want to take. So I chose another path: a path that looked at my life-style and my world-view. One of the strategies suggested was to have a 'conversation' with the pain; to have a relationship with it rather than fighting it and being desperate to be free from it.

The Pain

Who are you? You who cause me so much pain; so much anguish
You are becoming stronger – I am becoming weaker
You are becoming more invasive. You are more powerful than ever before
I have tried to ignore you. I have tried to deny you
I have tried to believe 'that's it' – nothing more can be done
I have allowed no space for the answer to 'who are you?'
So... who are you?

I am the seed within you. I am YOU. We are one
You already know this – yet you still deny it
I am your higher Self – your consciousness – this is the way to you now
Without me – your pain – would you be 'working' so hard, reflecting as much, learning as much?

A seed – your Seed – needs nurturing
You do not take care of yourself – until you do I cannot grow easily
Until you love yourself how can you love?
Until you love and accept yourself – including me – how can you accept others fully?
I bring you opportunities
Opportunities to transform your demons
Opportunities to begin to approach your destiny
Opportunities to find love and use your power, your heart, your spirit

Heather Tweddle

Coming to a Full Stop

It was not long after this that I made one of the hardest decisions I'd ever made – I stopped work. This gave rise to important issues of identity. Who was I? I was no longer a teacher; no longer a massage practitioner or counsellor. I had no job at all. I'd lost my physical well-being. I wasn't a wife or a mother. Who was I? I hit a very dark, low point in my life.

In addition to all that, my condition is an invisible one. I know I can look really well and healthy whilst feeling a lot of pain and drained of any spark of physical energy. I found this incredibly frustrating at times. I would at least get sympathy and greater understanding if, say, I had a limb in plaster or, in my darker moments, if I had a serious, or even terminal, illness. There were also those who said I simply had to 'get on with it'; make myself do the work and then I would feel better. This fuelled the despair, the isolation and my low sense of worth.

Through many conversations and healing sessions, and much reflection and meditation, I began to recognise that this is exactly what had led me to this situation in the first place. My determination to keep going, my inability to distinguish between being ill and simply a 'little tired', and my inability (refusal) to give in to injuries or weariness had all played key roles in the physical collapse that followed.

I had pushed myself beyond normal endurance expectancies. My life had been non-stop, especially after Neil's death when I became frenetic for a while – all unconsciously avoiding addressing the real issue. Gradually I began to see that my lesson in all this was to stop. I had ignored so many messages in the form of injuries and through pushing myself to and beyond what I knew was my physical limit, so I received an injury that I simply could not ignore. I really had no choice. I had to stop and I had to re-evaluate just about every aspect of my life. This gave rise to a number of key questions for me.

So Many Questions

How come I drive myself so hard?

How come I can't give myself permission to slow down?

Where does my sense of identity come from?

Is it from what I do or is it from who and how I am?

What will I become if I have to stop on a permanent basis?

Where will all this take me?

What will I do?

If I stop working for a living, how will I, can I, survive financially?

Heather Tweddle

In exploring these questions I became aware that the injury was a gift to me in a bizarre way. It was only because I was forced to stop physically that I have had the space and spaciousness to take on what I now know to be my true journey. It has only been since I left conventional paid employment that I have learned so much more about the value of stillness; the wonder of just sitting with a tree, by a river, in my garden, in an Abbey, with an other, with a group – all with intent.

I also came to recognise another, even greater, gift. The nature of Neil's death meant that the company for which he worked pays me a monthly pension. This is what enabled me to do what I now knew I had to do – stop and re-assess everything in my life. I would need to be careful but it was possible. Here was his final gift to me.

As I gained these insights and changed my lifestyle to one of more contemplation and stillness, the symptoms eased. I know my body is not as strong as it once was, and I have learned (and still need reminders occasionally) to manage my levels of energy so much better. My priorities have changed so that I now am able to take on those things that seem most important and appropriate at any given point. I have learned how to say 'No' more easily and with less guilt. I learn more each day about the power of 'being', rather than constantly doing, so I have time for reflection, for the stillness of the mind.

The Deficit Economy

Another big part of my work in the Shadowlands concerned the 'deficit economy'. For me, the deficit economy contained the belief that other people were always more important; that their needs were always to be put before mine and should be met first. I also found it difficult to believe that I had 'enough'; enough money, acceptance, skills, gifts or a place in another person's life. I believed that there was only so much of anything to go round and that I would be the one who would be left wanting. I believed, too, that I could never be as loved as others. When a new person arrived in an other's life then the belief told me I would automatically be pushed further down the line or even out of the picture altogether. It was as though I believed there was a limit to love and that it would be used up before it reached me; there would be none left for those (me) at the bottom of the heap of some imagined hierarchy.

Comparisons are a particularly poisonous aspect of this pattern. It led me to imagining all kinds of slights that did not exist; it led me to see endings of relationships that weren't there; it led to times of anguish and pain that were, in reality, unnecessary. Dropping the comparisons and the fantasies I would create of how I perceived others' relationships to be was a major step in moving beyond this particular pattern. I came to understand and accept that if my relationship with the other person is how I wish it to be and it gives both of us what we need then that is what is important; the relationship they might have with anyone else is none of my business. It was a major shift in perspective that released me from the grip of envy and jealousy; something that had held me trapped and power-less for some time.

Another shift began when, during a session, Bryce asked me what I considered to be a huge amount of money to spend without causing me financial difficulty. I said £600; he then challenged me to spend £800. There were certain conditions: I could only buy non-essentials i.e. no food or household necessities or anything I actually needed for running my home, and I was not 'allowed' to spend more than 5p either side of the £800.

This was a challenge indeed. It meant spending on me; shopping for what I would *like* rather than what I needed. I had no idea what to buy; I had little sense of what I wanted. In the event I accepted the challenge and went to town – with a friend – and spent £800.01! It was great and I really enjoyed showing Bryce what I had bought. I haven't stopped shopping since – within my own limits of course!

It was an amazing experience; it helped me shift out of the narrow restrictions I placed on myself and it began the process of valuing myself and loving myself. When I no longer need to look to others for my sense of who I am, my sense of belonging, my sense of worth, I am able relate to others freely and with fewer of the driven elements that so frequently controlled my interactions and way of behaving in groups.

Being Me

I am learning that wherever I am, whoever I am with, whatever the task
I can be; I can be Me

This is wonderful, scary, liberating, powerful and amazing
There is less conflict within when I am me

When I am in myself and when I accept myself, there is a serenity, a sense of peace I have rarely experienced
When I am in this place there is a sense of love for myself and I am able to receive love
When I love myself I have less need of approval/attention from others

It is a good place to be!

Heather Tweddle

3

Walking in Freedom

Introduction

The moments of illumination, transition points and insights were peppered throughout my time in the Shadowlands, but none of them would have occurred if I had not faced my 'dark night of the soul' – which was not a single experience. It was only by being willing to face those demons of fear, terror, isolation, loss of sense of identity, lack of self-worth, amongst others, that I began to feel my way through and beyond the Shadowlands. There came a point when I suddenly realised I was no longer in that place and I felt like a released prisoner. I was free, yet in a world that seemed strange and different, and with a new and different me to get to know too.

Of course there was still work to do – there always will be. There were still times when I fell off my perch, as I call it when a pattern jumps up and catches me unawares, but this was happening less and less. Further, I was able more regularly to feel that joy I experienced when the terror first flowed away from me. I began to look at issues and themes because I chose to, because I was interested in them or because it felt the right step to take rather than being plummeted into places of such darkness that I had to work hard to escape. It was also a time of recognising how much

I had shifted and how far I had travelled. It was and is a time of celebration and wonder.

The following concepts and ideas have each, in their own way, been integral to my emergence from the Shadowlands and enabled me to take on my mantle as a warrior and step onto the pathless path that was waiting for me with a degree of freedom I never knew was possible.

Claiming my Power

The experience in Bryce Canyon, described in the previous chapter, instilled in me an unfamiliar feeling of power. Not of physical power or of having power over objects or other people, but a sense of my own place in the universe and my own sense of me in the world. It was such an empowering time. I still had much work to do around patterns and my shadow yet it became clearer that power – how I expressed power, and how I experienced others using their power – was an underlying thread and the very essence of *going soul-o*.

Freedom

Growing into my own power was fundamental in my route to freedom; freedom to be more of who I am destined to be; freedom to be able to say no – or yes – if it is appropriate for me at this time and in these circumstances. Being in my own power leads to freedom from an anxious neurosis about whether I will be liked or loved if I take a certain course of action. Being in my own power both enables me to be heard and gives me the space to listen to others. Growing into my own power leads to the vanquishing of fear that, in turn, leads to letting go of a driven need to know the precise outcome of a course of action or a decision before embarking upon it – an important element of the spiritual life.

When I am not invested in getting my own way because I need to feel in control, or because I need to feel I have 'done' something to help another, or because I have to prove something to somebody else, then I can simply bring myself to these situations. This leads to greater confidence in new or different circumstances, which is an invaluable asset in a journey into the unknown! It also led me to being able to see more options and making **free** choices. With this came the ability and the capacity to take responsibility for my own thoughts, beliefs, values, stances and actions.

Being in my own power, though, is not another guise for 'power over', far from it. Being in my own power enables me to let go of having to be right, or of always getting my own way, or of always being the one to have the last word, or the first.

> "The final and possibly the greatest risk of love is the risk of exercising power with humility."
>
> **M Scott Peck,** *The Road Less Travelled,* p161. Arrow, 1990.

Neither is being in my own power a cause for arrogance. Humility goes with personal power and is actually more likely to be the accompanying quality; wearing the mantle lightly is an indication of someone who is truly in their own power. It gives rise to a stance that does not expect anything less of anyone else; a stance that does not expect others to do as you say; a stance that does not expect to be superior to another. Being in my own power in an aware and conscious manner has had a profound effect on how I exercise power around others and in the world in general.

Loving Acceptance

The capacity to be 'me' and the awareness of my power and how I use it, abuse it or give it away, are crucial in how I relate to others. I now know that I am called to travel in relationship with others, in relationship to my communities, in relationship to the planet so that I become more fully who I was born to be. I have moved away from my belief that love would not come my way freely and that love has to be earned by pleasing, by being right, by being what or how the other person needs me to be. I now have a very different understanding and experience of love i.e. the acceptance of people wholly and completely for who they are. There are no judgements and no pre-conditions; there are no limits to its scope and it is not a finite commodity. An integral part of being in relationship with other people, or with the Divine, is love of this quality.

I found experiencing that sense of acceptance regardless of who I am – actually because of who I am – as freeing and transformative. It was recognising that I was being offered such love and acceptance by another person that started the huge shift towards loving myself. Even more, it was amazing to be able to see that this love and acceptance was present in spite of what I saw as my 'unloveability' and in spite of the way I saw myself. It is something that is out of this world. It is an experience of nothing less than the universal love displayed through and manifested in other people.

> "To love another person is to see the face of God."
>
> **John R Yungblut,** quoted from *Les Miserables* in *Shaping a Personal Myth to Live By,* p77. Element, 1992.

Further, knowing that I was truly loved and welcomed in the universe by the universe was a magical, life enhancing experience. It is an experience I find difficult to describe yet one which is limitless in its power and influence. It challenged my sense of low esteem, self-worth and the belief that I had no right to live, that I wasn't fit to live. It raised the previously unthinkable, unimaginable prospect that I was worthy to live simply for being who I am. It gave rise to greater freedom; freedom to experiment and be less fearful of getting things 'wrong'. With less anxiety about making mistakes, I could take hold of more opportunities and challenges, and take more risks.

> "To live by love is to accept that all love – however profane or however spiritual – is a gift."
>
> **Carol Pearson,** *Awakening the Heroes Within,* p153. HarperSanFrancisco, 1991.

Loving myself then becomes a possibility – after all, if the universe/the Divine/God loves me, how can I presume that I know better and not love myself? This is a tremendous transition point: from being dependent on others in the world for my view of me, to looking to myself as the arbiter for how I feel about me, how I will act in the world and how I present myself to others.

恕

Forgiveness

With such love comes a greater sense of the realities of the human condition; the way in which I might strive yet not always get it 'right' – because I will hurt others by what I say or do, often unintentionally, but also intentionally, sometimes. With greater understanding of the human condition and of the power of love comes forgiveness; forgiveness of myself and of others.

I came to recognise that others were less hard on me than I was on myself for what I perceived to be faults and flaws that others could never accept. This led me to an increasing awareness of loving myself, of forgiving myself for mistakes made. It was learning to forgive myself, accepting that mistakes are 'normal' and that they are opportunities for growth and development, which led me to a place of greater compassion, understanding and acceptance of others.

> "...it is compassionate love that allows us to forgive the people we love for not living up to our image of them and for their inevitable inability to fulfil all our needs."
>
> **Carol Pearson,** *Awakening the Heroes Within,* p153. HarperSanFrancisco, 1991.

Being the Witness

Ram Dass tells a story of someone who was giving up the habit of smoking. He was doing really well; two weeks without buying tobacco. Then, one day he was busily saying his mantra only to realise he had gone into his shop and bought his tobacco without even realising it! He had lost his conscious awareness of what he was doing and operated out of habit; lost in how he used to be.

As I learned to be more aware of what I was doing each moment of each day, I developed the capacity to **witness** what I did. Simply being aware of what I am doing is not enough; I can be aware and yet be very *judgemental* of what I notice myself doing. Falling into criticism, guilt, feelings of inadequacy and inferiority only kept me locked in the habit, pattern or response that was causing the problem in the first place. It 'feeds' the behaviour, response or whatever the trigger is and gives it more power, which, in turn, increases its capacity to gain a stronger hold. Giving myself a hard time for repeating what I perceived to be 'undesirable' behaviour also takes a lot of energy; energy that can be more positively used to get myself 'back on track'.

Noting that I have reacted again in a certain way, for example, without judging or criticising myself for that particular behaviour, is a very different stance to take. Coming to recognise the triggers for these behaviours so that the pattern may be averted more easily and progressively more quickly is much more useful than some form of self-flagellation. Being a witness to my own actions is not, however, simply a way of excusing driven behaviours or stuck patterns; on the contrary, being a witness is an active process whereby behaviours are noted and, if necessary, are then focussed upon for further development, clarification and/or understanding.

Personal Responsibility

An outcome of having moved through the Shadowlands was stepping out of living by the expectations of others that I had taken on so well. This was a challenging step for me. It entailed continually monitoring myself in respect of what I believed, what I felt to be right and what I saw as being important.

I began to see that I had choices to make and, for a time, my life became that much more difficult as I struggled with so many choices, so many decisions to make and with taking so much more responsibility for my own life. My choices related to all manner of things but perhaps the greatest was the choice of how I view myself.

My Choices

What belief system, if any, do I wish to subscribe to?

How will I live my life?

What will my moral choices be?

What lifestyle choices will I make?

How will I perceive others and their value?

How will I view myself?

Heather Tweddle

When I live in the way I believe is expected of me, I fall into the roles and/or expectations society places on me and I become held and can feel trapped. Believing that I have choices to be who I wish to be rather than taking on others' demands, however well-meaning, is all about accepting personal responsibility for who I am, what I do, how I am in the world. I can then take hold of my own life and make all these choices for myself.

This can be an awesome responsibility, yet it is what being a self-determining individual is all about. It was crucial to understand that no one can 'make' me do anything and no-one can 'make' me feel anything – I only respond in the way I choose. Equally, no one can live my life for me; neither can anyone have *my* experiences. No one will ever have the same experiences – exactly. No one can tell me what will happen. No one can do it for me. Personal responsibility is everything.

Life Force

During this time, I was discovering another area of my life that is tremendously influential in enabling me to fulfil my potential in a truly complete way; the area of sensuality and sexuality. I came to realise that my attitudes towards sexuality were often not aware, conscious choices but rather were in-built reactions largely based upon social conditioning.

I thought of myself as an individual, but not as a woman; my sexual being was pretty much dormant and my passion was yet to be truly discovered. It has taken me a number of years to slowly step into my womanhood, sometimes with 'eureka' moments and sometimes with gentle realisations that a shift has been made.

The understanding I have gained through this dimension of my journey has been truly liberating and I now know that sexuality and spirituality are inextricably connected. They are not separate and distinct parts of me that are experienced separately; they are as closely linked as anything can be and are simply different manifestations of the same life force, energy or Chi, as the Chinese call it.

My first personal and clear encounter with this concept occurred some years ago as I was walking around Rievaulx Abbey. I suddenly felt flooded by that sense of connection with all that is; a feeling with which I was becoming more familiar. Yet this particular occasion had an added dimension because I had such a whole body response, beyond that of the spiritual/transpersonal experience, which was nothing less than the strongest orgasm I had experienced to that point in my life. The similarities were so marked that there could be no mistake; the distinguishing feature was the sheer intensity, totality and extent of the feelings.

Although I already had some intellectual understanding that the different aspects of my life are all linked and inter-dependent, this was an example of experiential learning far more powerful than any academic study! Feeling this unified expression of energy in its different forms simultaneously propelled me into a deeper level of awareness of the inter-connectedness and inter-dependence of all things. It was a magical and transformative experience.

It is easy to see why sexuality is something many religions seek to denigrate in some way or to put rigid and punitive boundaries around. Being aware of my own sexuality and the power inherent in that place leads to a level of self-empowerment that the establishment would find very threatening and a challenge to the status quo. Personal freedom, such as can be experienced and expressed through genuinely living comfortably in my body and sexuality, would do precisely that.

My exploration of the role of my sexuality within the spiritual became an integral part of my journey and was a major factor in the awakening of my whole being. This is more to do with the qualities of the archetypal feminine and masculine rather than my gender so, as I explored my sexuality and embraced more of my feminine qualities, I was aware that I also wanted to retain the valuable masculine qualities with which I was familiar. I began to relish the possibility for embracing both the feminine and masculine spirits within me with a conscious awareness so that I could grow towards greater wholeness.

> "The birth of the true Self always comes out of a marriage of the inner man and woman."
>
> **Carol Pearson,** *Awakening the Heroes Within,* p267. HarperSanFrancisco, 1991.

Death – Teacher and Friend

Running through much of my exploration has been the underlying theme of death and I was beginning to realise it was a topic in which I had developed a considerable interest. This 'morbid' fascination, as some might see it, was partly stimulated by the fact that it was death that had propelled me into this journey, and partly because I had been through times when I believed that the only step that made sense was to end my life.

Death is perhaps one of the last really taboo subjects in our culture and, in the West at the present time, death is largely hidden from view. Yet death is an integral part of life and Buddha is reported to have observed that of all the mindfulness meditations "that on death is supreme". It is too important to be left to chance or brushed aside to be looked at 'later' or 'when I have to'. Death is one of those events in life that can literally strike at any time, to anyone of any age or level of fitness. Developing my own relationship with death created yet more internal spaciousness and freedom thus enabling me to have more space for my journey into the unknown.

Birth is often, though not always, perceived as a happy, welcome event that is talked about and celebrated. Death, on the other hand, has an amazing number of euphemisms attached to it in order to avoid the very word itself. It's as though by not using the word, the concept and the reality can be shrouded, avoided or lessened to some degree. Yet it is by facing the starkness of it and by looking at what it means to me, to my view of the world, my life and what will happen after my death that I am liberated to live fully in the now.

Certain questions had been with me for some time: What does death mean to me? How do I feel about not existing in the world? What might my legacy be (particularly since I have no children)? I became particularly aware of death, especially my death, when I needed to have major surgery (I react very badly to anaesthetics and my fear was strong). I wrote the piece overleaf as part of my preparation for the operation.

Dying

Dying before I die; saying 'goodbye' before I leave
Ending before the end
A strange place to be in; thinking of tomorrow – what ifs!

What if – I die?
What if – I become a 'vegetable'?
What if – I can no longer function?
What if...?

What is my legacy to my friends; my family; the world; the universe?
I know I have touched many people's lives in many ways

Death – my death – is inevitable, although maybe not tomorrow.
Not the end – not even to be feared
Peace – acceptance; a strangely quiet, calm place

Trust in myself
Trust that fear is the only thing which keeps me from experiencing
fully and loving fully

Heather Tweddle

I also realised I had greater fears around old age and the manner of my death rather than actually being dead. I had many conversations around the topic, read books, meditated and then, in May 2005, I went on a journey; a guided shamanic[7] meditation on my own death. It was an awe-full experience; extremely powerful and intense.

---

[7] A shaman is "the one who sees in the dark" (Sandra Ingerman) and can be either a man or woman. Through journeying, shamanism forms a link between the visible world and an invisible spirit world for purposes of healing, divination, or related activities.

I was greeted at the entrance to my cave by two of my power animals and a shaman was waiting for me inside – someone I had 'met' before. He was smiling, serene and welcoming. I saw me die. I felt my death. I saw my body disintegrate. I saw what remained: a very small pile on the floor of the cave. I felt and saw me after death – my transcended Self; my ascended Self.

When I first 'came back', I wept for the loss of my body. Yet I also felt a profound sense of my body only being a vehicle for my essence; only a vehicle for my consciousness. I knew then that when the time comes to shed my body, my essence lives on.

Death is not Defeat

Death is not defeat
Death is not failure
Death is not the end
Death is not giving up
Death is not the final separation
Death is the beginning of another journey
Death is a joining
Death is a union/fusion with the Eternal
Death is knowing
Death is a completion
Death is not to be feared.

Heather Tweddle

I remained in a deep state for a considerable period and when, shortly afterwards, I was 'working' with someone else I knew that I was also fully present to that person. This was the first time I was aware consciously of being able to operate equally effectively from within two different states at the same time.

Over time, as I reflected on the experience, I also realised that my fear of old age had diminished as I gained a growing sense that if I focus on what might be then I am not with what *is*. If I am not with what is, then I lose what is. I also began to understand that I have the capacity to influence the time, place and manner of my own death, to allow the transcendence – if I am able to be in this open, connected space at that time.

> "Something in us still clamours for personal survival in some recognizable form, but there is also in us what there was in Jung – a 'still small voice' within that is willing to forego this last frenetic plea of the ego and to 'let go' with confidence and trust into the 'homecoming'."
>
> **John R Yungblut,** *Shaping a Personal Myth to Live By,* pp96-97. Element, 1992.

An understanding of death cannot change a physical condition and cannot prevent death, but it can enable me to live my life fully from day to day. Gaining a sense of detachment from death freed me from all those anxieties and concerns about when, how and so on that take such a lot of energy and space. I found I was spending time reflecting on such things as: What is it like for me to contemplate a world without me? How do I wish to plan/approach my own death? What do I want to do before that time? How would I choose to be remembered? Is that how I think others will remember me? Are there things I need/wish to say to others? How do I view what will happen to me after my death? These are all big questions but perhaps the greatest one is that last one. How I view what will happen to me after death will have an enormous impact on how I live my life now.

> "Death, then, looks both forward and back. Death is the pivot between two worlds..."
>
> **Zaleski & Kaufman,** *Gifts of the Spirit,* p248. HarperSanFrancisco, 1998.

The shamanic meditation on my death also served to deepen my understanding of life after death. This was not in the traditional Christian view of going to heaven for all time but much more in the sense of having a spirit, an essence, a soul, a consciousness (so many words in an attempt to describe something for which our language is insufficient) which continues for many life-times. I moved away from the notion of a heaven where I might go (if I met the criteria) and where I would meet loved ones who had already died – if they, too, met those criteria. This sense of a place – or even a state – where nothing more would change and where there is a kind of utopia from which many, many people are excluded no longer fitted for me.

The Circle of Life

I began to view life more as a cycle rather than as a linear, single experience, and the Circle of Life became a useful symbol for me. It is a universal symbol of cosmic unity, astrology, evolution. It is the pagan sacred circle; a Wheel of Life to Buddhists; a Medicine Wheel to Native Americans; a Mandala to Hindus. It symbolises unity, movement, the sun, the zodiac, re-incarnation, and the earth's cycles of renewal.

Living in the Moment

In all my searchings, seeking, explorations of the shadow, there was a phrase I found very helpful:

> I have a past but I am not my past.

When I came to understand that my past is part of me but that it does not have to control me now or in the future I felt a great sense of freedom. This awareness enabled me to find more of a balance between being absorbed in what has already happened and how come I am where I am, looking ahead to what might be, and focussing on the present. I learned that it is only by living in the present moment that I can live my life fully; neither held by the past nor always spending energy on what might be, especially if this is a fearful anticipation of what might be – as mine so often was.

Fearful anticipation was particularly present if I was going to be part of a group. I would move through a whole range of feelings that deeply affected my capacity to function and operate in the group – and not in a useful way. I would begin to feel incredible anxiety many days, even weeks, before the event, which then moved to fear that had the effect of severely restricting my options as I felt numbed and frozen. I held back, I isolated myself and so felt I was given one of the very things I feared – exclusion.

My huge learning was that, in a very real sense, the present moment is the only time I can influence and/or change and, even more, when I am able to operate from that moment there is no fear. It was a liberating and amazing place for me to find.

Living in the moment is closely linked to mindfulness (which is discussed more fully in the next chapter), yet there is a fundamental distinguishing feature between the two. Living in the moment can originate out of someone's ego; it can be from very selfish or self-centred motives. Mindfulness, on the other hand, transcends the ego and embraces a non-possessive openness to what is.

Living in the moment can occur in any situation. Let's take robbing a bank as an example! The bank robbers can be so focussed on their endeavour that they truly live in the moment. In fact, it would be dangerous for them to be anything less and would probably lead to mistakes, discovery and arrest. Mindfulness, however, has a very different quality embodied within it: it has nothing of self-interest within it; it comes from a place of non-attachment.

On a simple, practical level living in the moment is about focussing on the matter in hand, whether that is photocopying, shopping, washing the car, having a conversation, being part of a business meeting, or any of my myriad activities. It is about maintaining attention on the matter in hand at the level needed rather than, say, planning the evening meal, or what I am going to do tomorrow, or what shopping to do, or the conversation/argument I've just had, the last meeting, doctor's appointment – the list could be endless.

These are only examples as a way to highlight how easy it is (and natural) for my mind to wander from *this* moment to focussing on something that has already happened or something that has not yet happened. If my attention is split, how can I possibly bring everything to the task or activity in hand? I lose from it and the others lose also.

The Moment is Precious

NOW is the only 'time' we have
To wish 'now' away would be sad
'Now' can be lived (anywhere and everywhere)
'Now' can be felt
'Now' can be a breathing space; a time of transition from one experience to another
'Now' can be a time for reflection
It is not easy and it can be dangerous!
It can also be very, very precious

Heather Tweddle

Living in the moment is thus largely about being *present;* being present both to myself and to any others involved in the experience at that moment. It is about bringing myself in all my fullness into everything I do. This does not mean, however, that I am the same wherever I go, other than in bringing myself to all I do. I will, for example, be different in a school governors' meeting than a social encounter, yet in each I can be fully present.

This is a very powerful concept and much of my work on awareness could be said to be about learning how to live in the moment. It challenges me to live each experience fully and is closely linked to the concept of congruence, and it forms, for me, the bridge between the personal and the interpersonal, into the transpersonal.

> "Only by living in the Present can we experience the Living Presence that is not outside us and beyond reach, but within us every moment of an ever-present Now."
>
> **Kenneth Meadows**, *Where Eagles Fly,* p85. Element, 1995.

It is being in this place – of experiencing and accepting love, being able to forgive myself and others, living in the moment – that led me still further, deeper, higher into the world of spiritual exploration and discovery and along the Pathless Path.

4

The Pathless Path: Entering the Forest

> "The most beautiful and most profound emotion that we can experience is the sensation of the mystical." **Einstein**

Introduction

Embarking on the pathless path (a phrase from the wonderful quartet of books called *The Masks of God*, by Joseph Campbell) was the moment when the focus of my journey shifted; it moved from largely concentrating upon my intrapersonal and interpersonal issues to the transpersonal and spiritual. I had reached the point where I knew I had sufficient spaciousness and freedom within to take this on and a line from the film *The Return of the King* (the third part of *The Lord of the Rings* trilogy by Tolkien) encapsulates my 'call'.

> "Become who you were born to be."

The above statement was made to Aragorn – the King in waiting – as he was presented with the tools, chiefly a sword, by which he would fulfil his destiny. He was encouraged to accept who he truly was and to accept his role with all its attendant responsibilities and consequences. Here is someone who has been following a path already yet he has first to accept within himself the truth of his true nature before he can fulfil it. He has to feel it; *he has to live it for himself*.

This was a profound moment for me, regardless of the fact it was only part of a fictional story. It was like a knife – a sword maybe – straight through to my heart and it brought tears to my eyes. The phrase, 'become who you were born to be', stays with me still and has become a constant companion. It serves both as a reminder of my quest and as a 'call to arms' in the sense of commitment, dedication, and my priorities.

I, like Aragorn, have to *live* my journey; I have to find *my* way and this demands that I make a *wholehearted commitment* to that regardless of what I might encounter on the way.

From that moment I could no longer pretend that my experiences were happening 'to' me rather than taking responsibility for them. I also knew that I could no longer rely primarily upon spontaneous experiences but that I would now be consciously seeking to create the conditions to open myself to the universe and whatever that might bring. I must now acknowledge that my life was fundamentally different and live accordingly. I must also now take on that all the wacky and weird experiences (as I thought of them for quite some time) were actually the norm in my new being in the world. Now was the time for no longer hiding my light 'under the bushel'. I needed to be less diffident; less reticent about what I was learning, what I was experiencing.

Living the Journey

The journey can be heartbreaking
Much has to be shed; the vessel made clearer and cleaner
Much has to be faced; demons, devils, friends and enemies
Much has to be purged; purified by the flames of power of the universe itself

The way can be painful
The way can be besieged by trials and tribulations
Trials of all the elements: earth, wind, fire and water
Feeling fear, deserted, outcast, besieged, yet herein lies the bliss

The bliss of connection of new awareness
The bliss and hell of contacting all that is, all that was, all that ever shall be
The bliss and hell of feeling the pain of the Universe

Alone in the journey, yet never alone
My own path, yet there are guides, there are markers

The journey never-ending – in this life and beyond
The journey to gain – regain – my Self
The journey to live freely, lovingly, fearlessly

Heather Tweddle

It was also the moment when I knew this was to be the 'work' of my life. Here was my true work; this was to be the priority in my life. From here on in I knew I needed to continually be awake to possibilities, open to all around me and learn to be discerning about how I spent my time, and where I placed my focus.

This chapter looks at that shift and what it heralded, exploring: the challenge of stepping into the unknown; the way of the warrior; the sacredness of all beings and all things; moving authority from 'out there' to 'in here'; the concept and practice of mindfulness.

The Pathless Path

In contrast with the external authority often found in traditional faith systems or with gurus, the pathless path personifies the individual journey, the unique journey, the journey that only one individual can take. If I do not take hold of the journey that is mine, the gifts that are mine and mine alone, there will forever be a gap and my gifts will be lost to the cosmos.

The knights, in their quests, were called upon to enter the forest alone and if any attempted to follow where another had already trodden, his quest was immediately forfeit. When one of the knights isn't sure which way to turn and enters the forest in the footsteps of another knight he fails; he is dishonoured, disgraced. Now, perhaps that particular fate does not await me, but when I try to follow the path of another, the path is no longer mine and my journey is compromised. This is not being true to my own journey, my own unique destiny.

Courage

To enter the forest at a point where there are no visible tracks or paths is an act of courage and an act of true exploration. When I am courageous, I don't give up; I try new things; I admit mistakes. Courage is the strength in my heart. This is the aim yet, naturally, human fallibility is part of the equation too!

The pathless path is also pathless because it is created as I go along and I might only know which way to turn at the point of making that turn. I have little idea where I might end up and letting go of my need to know outcomes has been crucial in understanding that the destination is not the point of travelling but it is the journey itself that is important.

So often it is the end result of a course of action or a plan that is given the greatest attention – and, of course, on many occasions that is quite rightly so. However, when it comes to my spiritual life, this is not the case. This is not a race to some end point. This is not a competition to see who has the most wacky or way out experiences – as seems to happen in some areas of transpersonal explorations. This is not in order to 'get there' – wherever 'there' is. Rather, it is about the journey itself, living in the moment, being mindful and savouring it.

If I focus on an end result it is all too easy to miss the gems along the way. When I was much more physically fit than I am now, I went climbing, running and walking. The aim was usually to go as far, or as high, or as fast (or all three) as I possibly could. So it was usually head down and go. Nowadays, following the enforced need to slow down, if not actually stop, I see much more. There is time – and breath – to look around. There is room to take in the sounds of all that is around. There is a greater sense of connection with the area in which I am walking or sitting. Even though I cover far less ground in a literal sense, in another way I cover far greater ground because there is room in me to take in more: time to reflect; time to be part of what is happening around me; time simply to be.

The Sacredness of All

The idea that everyone is sacred was a major factor in my transition from the interpersonal elements of my journey into spiritual dimensions and propelled me onto the pathless path. I first became really aware of the vastness of this concept after one of those 'eureka' moments on a visit to a church during a personal retreat at Rievaulx Abbey. There was no one else in the church and initially I just wandered around, feeling an unexpected sense of unease. I felt drawn to the high altar and as I looked at the crucifix behind the altar an anguished question burst from me, 'Christ – who are you?' The answer was incredibly fast and so very clear:

'I am who you are.'

This was being said to me by Christ. I turned away. I couldn't hear that, yet I had that familiar feeling in my right hand and arm; the feeling I had first experienced in the ordination service in Ripon Cathedral all those years ago. A feeling which has proved pretty infallible. A feeling which signifies the importance, the truth, the validity of whatever is happening at this moment. Then, a transformation: what fabulous feelings; beyond my words to describe accurately. I felt so alive; more alive than I had ever felt in my life to that point. I felt such connection with others; other souls (like the children I could see, so free and real and alive and natural). I felt glad to be alive – and that was a pretty unique experience. There was a lightness in my step; walking tall and free.

I had a gut-wrenching 'light bulb' moment of understanding – Christ and I are one and the same. There is no differentiation between us in the sense of God and lesser being; no separation in the sense of sacredness or innate divinity; no difference in the sense of potentiality for connection with the Divine and being in touch with my own divinity. There was no escaping the truth of this. And, more to the point, there was no escaping the implications and consequences of this for how I live my life from this moment on.

I began to see that the uncomfortable feeling I'd first felt had been something to do with being known. That in this place there was no pretence, no hiding, no barriers. **All** my feelings were known and open and I was still loved; more than loved – 'I am who you are'. It was so hard to believe this. The powerful feelings, repressed and suppressed for so long, felt as though they would erupt like a flood or a volcano; so strong that others (and me) would be frightened off.

I learned that Christ is my 'daimon'. I began to understand 'I am in Christ and Christ is in me'. He is the example of someone in touch with himself, with those around him and with God. He followed his path. He was not swayed by others' thoughts of him or by others' fears or hatred of him. He followed his path with passion – yet not with arrogance or force or by being domineering. I was being called to walk a similar path.

> "There is that of God in every man and woman. Jesus differs from other men and women, not in kind, but in degree."
>
> **John R Yungblut,** *Shaping a Personal Myth to Live By,* p34. Element, 1992.

The experience completely challenged my view of me, of my relationship with God and my relationship with the man called Jesus Christ. I had the tremendous awareness that all beings are sacred; that everyone I meet is sacred. Everyone is equally divine. I also realised that if I truly accepted this, it must have a profound effect on how I relate to other people in every transaction I would ever have. This, of course, applied especially to those with whom I have a rather 'rocky' relationship and even more so to those I would actively avoid or disliked. If I was to live this new insight then it meant that I had to accept the sacred nature of others regardless of anything I had the temerity to observe or describe as 'wrong' behaviours.

A time of great reflection followed, which further deepened my sense of the sacredness of all. It intensified my awareness that I, we, all have the same potential, the same inherent sacredness and divinity, and I wrote this:

The Sacredness of All

Look into the eye of a child and look into the eye of the Divine
Look into the eye of the person you just passed in the street and look into the eye of the Sacred
Look into your heart and find the heart of the Beloved
All around in all things, in all people we meet the Divine

In the sky – birds winging and clouds scurrying
In the water – all living creatures
On the earth – the earth itself and all living things
In all the elements and in all creation there is the Divine, the Sacred

Heather Tweddle

The challenge for me was the realisation that if *all* beings are sacred, then, of course, it meant I was too and I had to begin the process of accepting my own flaws – my own blind spots. In many ways, I had no difficulty accepting this for others but it was harder to accept it for me.

Crucially, one of the things that I took from this experience was that I needed to relate to other people on a level deeper than superficial behaviours. We each have a soul; we each have the same divine essence within. We all, also, have behaviours overlaid on top of that which are the result of experiences, upbringing and so on. These are not to be simply discounted, but they become less of a barrier for compassion, for love, for understanding to flow from one sacred being to another.

> "Walk cheerfully over the world; answering that of God in everyone."
> **George Fox**

Thus I was beginning to experience for myself the essence of the saying 'love the sinner and not the sin'. Not a phrase I would usually choose to use but a good example of something I have always subscribed to intellectually but which I now felt deeply in my being.

I was challenged to take this understanding yet further when I visited San Francisco and went across to Alcatraz. It is a fearsome looking island surrounded by dangerous tides and subject to fog rolling in and out of the Bay in most unpredictable ways. It was possible to hear the fog-muffled sounds of the city and yet have absolutely no sight of it at all. There was an incredible sense of isolation and, as I walked the tour, there was a point when I had such a connection with the prisoners. I felt their suffering and experienced an unexpected compassion for them regardless of what had brought them there. It felt really strange since I have no sympathy for rapists, murderers and the like – always believing that they get what they deserve. Yet here I was, with what felt like a link to their deep humanity; the part of them that, maybe, is lost, is inaccessible to them, that is buried underneath all that happens on the sensory, surface level.

Another, similar experience was a spontaneous inner response whilst hearing a woman on the radio talk about McVeigh – a convicted criminal who had been on Death Row in the US for many years. He had been executed that morning. She wanted him to have a tortuous death – he had committed some horrendous crimes against people – and not the "simple, easy" death she perceived the State was allowing him, but there was a strange sense in me that no-one should die like this, although I could not – would not – condone his actions.

I felt an unexpected and profound sadness and compassion towards him. How could this be possible? Because I knew that at his very core he also was a sacred being. This compassion was for his Self; a Self that must have been sorely damaged at some time. It was a position that felt pretty alien to me at the time yet it was clear, it was strong and it felt right and loving.

I took all this into many discussions and reflections about vengeance, about justice and – primarily – personal responsibility. Where is the line drawn when talking about taking responsibility for one's own actions; for example, if an individual cannot, or will not, do this then is it acceptable to look for possibilities of retribution or does that simply become vengeance? It raised many questions for me that I still reflect upon and feel challenged by.

These experiences really challenged me to take on the understanding that the flaws I perceived in others were irrelevant to their sacredness. My horizons were expanding and my views of God/the Divine were being radically changed as I came to see that there is that of the Divine in all of us. God is not just something that comes in from outside us if a request is made and certain conditions are met, such as asking for forgiveness and so on. It is inside already. It is our innate state and it is our true nature, but it is one that we lose/forget. All things are sacred; all is divine. My journey is about growing back into this true nature.

Mindfulness

正念

Mindfulness

The idea of living a life of mindfulness followed on so naturally from the revelation about my inherent sacredness and the sacredness of others. For me, mindfulness is about a whole life, a whole body response and way of being. It is about staying in my own power, neither giving it away to others nor using it abusively. It includes the notion of being the witness to my own life whilst also recognising that everything, every single thing, I do is equally important. It is about bringing mindfulness into all I do, all I say, all my decisions, my whole world. It is about being aware of what is happening around me – in the way of being sensitive rather than a neurotic worrying of what is or might be happening.

Mindfulness entails a *conscious and aware being* in every second of my life. It is an ideal that I am unlikely to attain all the time until I become an enlightened being, but it is one which I can endeavour to live more and more.

> "The 20th century Quaker Tomas Kelly writes of immersing oneself in the 'eternal now', which we experience as 'a steadfast presence, an infinite ocean of light', by which we see all human beings in a new way, as brothers and sisters, as children of God."
>
> **Zaleski & Kaufman,** *Gifts of the Spirit*, p18. HarperSanFrancisco, 1998.

In order to be mindful of others I must first be mindful of my own inner reality. In order to be mindful of my own inner reality I must be willing to look into myself and it is in looking into myself that I can open myself to so much more around me – and this is what the journey is all about.

In my experience, and that of countless others, mindfulness practice is part of a transpersonal and spiritual dimension and powerfully holds within it the capacity to take me yet deeper into myself, to connect with the Divine. Used in this context, mindfulness is a particularly deep form of meditation; meditation that has no pre-conceived outcome, no purpose other than itself. This is not to say that the practice of mindfulness is lax or haphazard; far from it, great discipline and commitment is needed to follow the path of mindfulness.

> "Buddhists everywhere practise the discipline of mindfulness, wherein one strives to be engaged in the present moment for the purification of beings, for the overcoming of griefs and sorrows ... for winning the right path, for realising Nirvana.
>
> The basic form of meditation that the early texts describe the Buddha as teaching is not sitting meditation, as one might have expected from modern formal practice, but something to be done by a monk as he 'fares along', going about his normal business. It consists of the specific applications of Mindfulness."
>
> **Zaleski & Kaufman,** *Gifts of the Spirit,* p19. HarperSanFranciso, 1998.

Mindfulness, then, is a means to understand things as they are and, according to Suzuki Roshi[8], it requires no special effort. His view is that we can simply register events as they occur: we don't analyse, we observe. So, when a reaction arises, whether it is intellectual, emotional, or physical, it is viewed as just another event in the stream of life, and a mindful attention to things as they are continues. I learn to notice if one of my patterns returns

[8] Shunryu Suzuki Roshi is the Zen master who founded the San Francisco Zen Centre and the Zen Mountain Centre in Monterey County, California, America's first Zen Monastery.

to me, but I am not 'hooked' by it, and so I do not give it extra power by talking about it obsessively or feeling how 'awful' I am for being caught 'again'. In turn, this enables me to recognise the signs of my patterns earlier and earlier so I can step aside.

The Search for the Holy Grail

Historically, the Holy Grail has been viewed as an artefact, the chalice that Jesus used. This may in fact be the case, yet it is one of those mysteries and myths that may never be proved one way or the other, and it may never be found. What is known, however, is that many, many people throughout the centuries have searched for this Holy Grail.

Yet there is another search for the Holy Grail: my search for continual mindfulness, and for connecting with others from the sacred space whilst remaining open to the Divine, is my quest for the Holy Grail.

For me, the Holy Grail is not a single object but a life-long quest for learning: learning about my relationship with the Divine; learning about my place in the universe; learning more about me; learning more about my role, my calling in this life. I view the Holy Grail as a transformative, healing eternal power which works from within and not an external object from which to receive power and eternal life.

So, the journey for the Holy Grail is the Holy Grail itself; it is a quest into the unknown and a leap of faith – taking each step as it presents itself and moving forward with courage, trust and faith. It is a quest to bring the unseen into the seen and the unknown to known.

The Quest for the Holy Grail

Each questor has to find/travel their own path, their purpose

The Beloved will seek you; your path will be shown to you
Your guides, your mentors, your familiars, will be made known to you
All you have to do is look and see; hear and listen; blow with the wind
All you have to have is courage and obedience and love
All you have to be is open, willing

Seek by being; teach by being; learn by being in all you do

Be and you will be your Holy Grail

Heather Tweddle

The intentions, the discoveries, the enlightenment and growth as I undertake this quest are what form the Holy Grail. Like a candle, the journey may flicker at times: sometimes it will burn brightly and clearly; at other times it may be a gentler, more subdued flame – resting, waiting. The quest of the Holy Grail is my struggles, my ups and downs. Life lived – life explored. Life grasped – life shared. Life *felt*.

Stepping into the Unknown

精

The spirit of a Warrior

The essence of embarking upon the pathless path and seeking the Holy Grail is stepping into the unknown. Making a commitment to such a path is the *way of the warrior*; a universal archetype that, over the centuries, has appeared in most of the world's spiritual traditions. The warrior steps into the unknown; follows what he (or she, of course) knows to be his (her) path without knowing what the outcome might be. Following the true path for the warrior is the most important thing in their life; holding fast to the 'dream' essential.

The way of the warrior represents the utter commitment of the person to the path they have chosen; it indicates the courage that is usually required to begin and continue the path; it highlights the possibilities for meeting obstacles and trials along the way; it represents the capacity for adapting to the circumstances that the warrior meets. A warrior is not an automaton on a fixed track that cannot be changed but is someone with a strong intent to "follow their own bliss", as Joseph Campbell describes it, whilst being open to new insights, new information, new experiences, the novel and the different.

To step into the unknown I needed *courage*, to transcend natural anxieties about what lay ahead; I needed *commitment* to myself, to my journey; I needed *detachment* or disinterest (not uninterest) in where the experiences or explorations might take me. Even as I began to feel drawn to explore realms and possibilities previously unknown or alien to me, it meant that I was embarking on a journey into the unknown.

> "The seeker's journey requires courage to break away from dependency and leap ahead into the unknown."
>
> **Carol Pearson,** *Awakening the Heroes Within,* p42. HarperSanFrancisco, 1991.

I am frequently reminded of that step Indiana Jones takes from the cliff in search of the Holy Grail, in the adventure film of the same name. This may seem a lightweight comparison for such a profound topic, yet it is a marvellous example of stepping out in trust. When I ignore the obvious fact that he had read the script and look at it symbolically, Indiana Jones trusted his instincts, had the courage to step out into what was a void, with no visible way of avoiding plummeting into the depths to his death. However, as those who have seen the film will know, a stone bridge appears out of nowhere – apparently – and he is able to walk safely across the chasm to find the Holy Grail. (Of course, that was not the end of his challenges, just as it isn't with the spiritual path.)

Stepping into the Unknown

What will I be like if I accept, believe, do this?

How will the people around me respond to this change in me?

How will my wider world be different?

Will I like the new me?

Will it be a permanent change or a temporary blip?

Can I do this?

How do I do this?

If I do this – what next?

Heather Tweddle

The feeling of taking a leap into the unknown, stepping off a cliff, being overcome by waves, being overwhelmed in some way is not an uncommon feature of the spiritual quest!

Stepping into the unknown is never more present than when I make a commitment to enter the realms of the spiritual, the transpersonal, the 'other'. I can never know what I might encounter. I can never know what I might experience. I can never know how my life might be affected by those encounters and experiences. I can never know who and what I might become. Further, I can never know how all this will affect the people around me, and this can be a deterrent to stepping fully into the unknown.

By its very nature, the unknown engenders a plethora of feelings and emotions – excitement, cautiousness, fear, dread and anticipation. I found I had two common reactions. I either froze and became incapable of doing/saying/feeling anything, or I jumped in impetuously with little or no awareness. I had to discover a place of balance and move beyond those opposites; to remain centred and trust my new-found sense of safety from within.

Sometimes I felt as if I was in a kind of no-man's land, where an old belief had been left behind but I hadn't yet found my new way of being. On occasion, this left me feeling so confused that I almost wished I had not left the old ways behind yet this confusion also provided an opportunity for a very real evaluation: evaluation of what I want in my life, who I want around me, the activities (if any) I wish to be involved with, what *my* world-view is – rather than a set of beliefs I have inherited or acquired from others along the way.

Stepping through or over such a threshold is awe-some. This has not been a one-off, once only phenomenon. I have experienced many occasions where I have, for example, needed to take on a new understanding that has implications for my life without knowing what the consequences might be. Stepping into that unknown is an act of faith and an act of courage.

From External to Internal Authority

The pivotal moment in stepping into the unknown and following the pathless path came when I decided to leave my role as Reader and step out of the Anglican Church. This allowed me to focus fully upon my more personal, more solitary journey, honouring my own inner authority. I began questioning my place in the Church as long ago as 2003 when events began to occur in the parishes that made it very clear I no longer needed to be there and, more, that it no longer felt the right place for me to be. I finally made the decision to leave in July 2006, officially stepping down in September of that year.

From the time of my 'desert' onwards, I began to understand that having fixed views and beliefs is not the sign of a strong faith but a sign of rigidity, inflexibility and fundamentalism. Yet in all of the new experiences and the beginnings of losing what I felt to be unbreakable 'truths' (as advocated by the church), I rarely lost the sense of the Divine, the Beloved, God: that presence which transcends my own narrow world; that transcends and unites all things. As my journey continued, I came to recognise its influence in so many ways and the writing opposite emerged during one time of reflection.

Whilst I honoured and recognised – and do still – the Christ path, there was a huge amount of the dogma and the rules of the Church of England with which I struggled. Increasingly, there was a clash between my own experiences and what the Bishops and other such dignitaries were saying was 'The Truth'. In practice, the existing church model demands that the external authority of priest, bishop, archbishop in a strong hierarchy outweighs personal experience – if such experience challenges the orthodoxy. Trusting my own experience, listening to my inner voice, was rarely encouraged.

The Divine

You have revealed yourself in so many ways
When I felt alone, empty, You nudged me
When I gave up looking there You were
When I stopped there You were
You always had been; You always are; You always will be

You cajole, challenge, chase....
You comfort, caress....
In all things You are there – when the veil falls from the eyes
In all people You are there – when I allow them You

You open me to new worlds
You touch me in mind, body, spirit

You and I are one
One in Spirit; one in Body

Heather Tweddle

And herein lies the key – **my own experience.** Authority very much came from 'above' in the Church yet I was now beginning to have experiences which were, apparently, beyond anything acceptable to the established, traditional Church. I moved inexorably, almost unnoticed at first, towards the point where I was no longer willing or able to deny the power and the authenticity of my own experiences. If they were not acceptable to the 'authorities' then I was not willing to 'toe the party line' any more in these areas.

One of the areas of dogma that caused me the greatest struggle was the strongly held belief that only Christians are on the 'true' path so, whilst others can be respected, 'we' know they actually are deluded. This idea of there being only one way to seek the divine and that everyone else was excluded from some form of heaven just no longer fitted for me.

In a similar way, the notion that only Jesus is divine no longer worked for me. I had had far too many vivid images and experiences, in church, at Rievaulx, in so many places, that informed me that we are all sacred, that we all have the potential to be as Jesus, still to believe that one.

Further, I came to realise that it was completely irrelevant to me whether there was a virgin birth or not. I'm not saying there wasn't; I'm not saying there was. It simply no longer mattered. It is the life of Jesus that is the key for me rather than how he came into the world.

In addition, the Creed, which was said in every service, is a man-made construct dating only from the fourth and fifth centuries, and it felt to be just that – constructed to serve men rather than an organic evolving of the teachings of the life of Jesus.

Past life experiences were common and perfectly acceptable to the Church at one time, but nowadays they are regarded with suspicion and criticism. Many of my past life experiences were mind blowing and painful, physically and emotionally, yet without exception they have provided valuable insights and have usefully informed my journey. How could this be 'wrong'? How could this be 'heretical'? And even if these images and events were not really another life I realised it did not matter. Even if they were simply my own inner imagination, my own inner wisdom, I was still learning a huge amount about me, about how I operate in the world and how come my life has been the way it has.

I met other beings; had awareness of other realms; saw the sacredness and Christ-power potential in all beings. None of these were acceptable and all were seen as heresy and delusional, at best.

Being told that such experiences and reflections are dark, heretical, and even 'the devil's work' challenged me to consider more deeply what I truly believed. The Church therefore did me a great service because I wrestled with these topics much more closely than I would have done if the authorities had not challenged me in any way. It gave me a stronger sense of what I do believe, what I don't; what I can accept and what I can't.

Once I had stepped out of the Church I felt so much freer; another aspect of the prisoner released. It gave me space and freedom to find *my* way, to explore and discover what *I* believe, find those ideas *I* am willing to stand up and out for, to work out *my* priorities and to take increasing responsibility for more aspects of my life.

5

Wild Encounters

Introduction

The extra-ordinary encounters and experiences I had from the very beginning of my awakening had been instrumental in pushing me into recognising there was a very different kind of journey beckoning me. They are the bedrock of my learning and my development. They open new vistas, new horizons and offer challenges to my way of thinking and operating. Above all, they were the impetus for examining my assumptions and my world-view. As I moved through the Shadowlands and stepped into greater freedom and personal responsibility this aspect of my journey took on a whole new importance and place in my life.

These experiences left me with many questions about what I was finding, feeling, seeing and living. What is real in my world? What is real in society? Are my dreams real? Is my intuition, my gut reaction real? What really exists? Are there different realities about which there is little or nothing known? Are there really other beings around me in a different dimension? Does time – past, present, future – exist in the same moment? This chapter focuses on these kinds of questions and my experiences in connection with them.

Reality: What is Real?

The above questions may seem more like science fiction and smack of Star Trek yet they were very real to me. My questioning led me to doubt my sanity on occasions and also to wonder where all this was taking me. There were certainly things I did not understand and couldn't make sense of in my rational, logic-based world.

For example, I remember an occasion in 1997 when I was in Carberry, Scotland, for a week-long workshop with Eric Cassirer (an international figure in healing). One of my challenges was a simple question from Eric about a magnificent tree we could see through the window. He asked me, 'What do you see?' My reply, unsurprisingly, was, 'A tree'. He then talked about perceptions and seeing what we are trained or conditioned to see, and that we only see an oak tree (in this case) because that's what we've been told it is.

I was perplexed; I didn't understand. Obviously it is a tree – and a very specific type of tree at that; I could see it clearly. It took me some time and many of my own experiences to come to some understanding of what Eric was saying. I realise that this is how I view the world now: there are many other ways of 'seeing'; there are many realities and beings that are outside and beyond the world as it is commonly viewed. It was only when I made this connection a year or two later that I remembered the conversation with Eric and I wrote the piece below.

Reality

What is 'reality?'
Something which can be seen, felt, experienced, proved?
Something which is common to all people?

Reality is meant to be concrete
Reality is meant to be safe
Reality is meant to be unchanging
This is no longer my experience of reality

Reality is individual; my reality may not be your reality
My perceptions, my responses are mine – they create my reality
Your perceptions create your reality
The two may be the same sometimes
The two may be different

I live in different realities; I have more than one life – now

Heather Tweddle

Another experience took me further into this exploration. Two spirit beings appeared in front of me (I 'knew' that is what they were even though at that time I did not have the words to describe them). I sensed nothing but love, compassion and interest from them, yet my instinctive reaction was one of fear – fear of the unknown, fear of what was going to happen, fear of what I would be expected to do and fear of being found wanting in some way. How could this be real? Was it my imagination? Was this another indication of impending insanity? In the event, they led me, very gently, to a different realm, a different reality. They showed me that there is knowledge, there are insights and experiences, to be gained from this kind of connection with the collective unconscious that I am called to bring back in order to teach others and help them with their awakening.

I had the strongest, clearest awareness that the past, the present and the future are all in me, all at the same time. They are not separate; time is not linear but cyclical. This shook my previously held certainties concerning the clear demarcation between those time periods. Isn't it obvious that the future hasn't happened yet; that the past is gone and cannot be changed? This is something that can be difficult to explain since the feelings and knowings are, once again, beyond the traditional rational logic of language in common use.

All my assumptions and all my preconceived certainties – for that is what they were – were being challenged. It became clear that my past does have a role; although events cannot be changed, my view of them, my understanding of them, my way of relating to them, are all within my influence. So my past is not there to hold me in old patterns, it is not there to keep me 'safe' in familiar yet unwise or outdated behaviours, but is there to inform, to teach.

火

Fire

I also learned how the present is a crucible: all parts of me were to be fully experienced and 'burned' i.e. refined, transformed, cleansed in the fire of the crucible. At the same time I 'saw' that the future is dark, in the sense of unknown; my future a pathless path; my crusade the search for the Holy Grail, to recognise, acknowledge and release my potential.

Altered States of Consciousness

I view a non-ordinary state quite simply as one that takes me out of my normal way of seeing things or perceiving the world around me.

> "An altered state of consciousness for a given individual is one in which he clearly feels a qualitative shift in his pattern of mental functioning, that is, he feels not just a quantitative shift (more or less alert, more or less visual imagery, sharper or duller, etc.), but also that some quality or qualities of his mental processes are different."
>
> **Charles Tart (Ed),** *Altered States of Consciousness*[9], pp1-2
> HarperSanFrancisco, 1990.

My experiences of altered states, non-ordinary states and heightened states began almost from the very outset of my awakening and they steadily increased in frequency and variety until they became my 'normal' experience. I experienced shifts in awareness of time where an experience appeared to last seconds and yet a much longer time had elapsed, or vice versa; I experienced spatial acuity shifts in how I literally saw things; I experienced variations in my sense of hearing, in all my senses and in my whole body. I saw the world in brighter, deeper colours, in much greater detail, and saw things that I had quite simply not noticed before.

Another of my experiences is simply 'knowing' (without knowing how I know) that a certain person is going to telephone me in the next few minutes. There are more and more occasions of such synchronicity; events that, perhaps, I would have once dismissed as coincidence. I am able to link into the presence of others and I am able to move into other states of being with greater ease as I continue with my journey and create that spaciousness within myself.

---

[9] This book is an excellent resource for studying the whole area of altered states of consciousness.

One early example of this knowing was when I was in the Chapel of St John's Theology College in Durham in 1993. I was there for an interview as a prelude to entering ordination training and all candidates were expected to attend the evening service. Across the chapel from me was a young woman and I knew that her father had a serious health issue, that he had some form of cancer. I later heard that she had only discovered this news herself earlier that week. I have no rational explanation for how I knew this, only that I did with a certainty I rarely experienced in the 'normal' realm.

Although so much of this seems to be beyond the ordinary, in some senses altered states are given a status way beyond what they deserve. The sacred, the awareness of all things, awareness of other states of being, awareness of other realms of existence are all part and parcel of our day-to-day lives. I see no separate compartment or area reserved for 'special' people, times, places, rituals. There are, of course, places that are more conducive for some people; there are certain rituals that enhance the state; there are certain times that draw us more closely; there are some people who seem more easily to enter altered states. However, I have found it important not to surround the whole concept with a mystique that keeps it separate from my whole being.

I have used many ways of entering altered states, including drumming, meditation, mindfulness practice, deep breathing, exercise, chanting, card readings, sitting, tai chi, yoga and reading – and there are many more. As altered, non-ordinary states became more familiar and more common in my life, I realised that I was no longer switching from one state to another like an on/off switch, and I no longer needed to use any particular method to find a way in. All the states are there in my consciousness; they all are equally accessible. The only decision then is to bring the state or states most relevant and appropriate to any particular moment and situation into the forefront of my awareness.

Entering altered states gives me moments of knowing about things, ideas and concepts that feel to be quite beyond my imagination, yet here they are – new understanding, insights, feelings and levels of consciousness.

Transpersonal/Spiritual Experiences

As I increasingly lived within this world, I began to explore more deeply where and how unconscious and altered states fit with transpersonal and spiritual experiences. Are altered states always transpersonal experiences? Is the spiritual dimension always present in any form of out of the ordinary experiences? At present, I view altered states of consciousness as forming a kind of umbrella category within which there are many forms of experience: transpersonal experiences being one, spiritual another, and transpersonal experiences need not be spiritual in their nature.

I am using 'transpersonal' to suggest any experience that takes me beyond myself into wider realms, enhancing the awareness of my whole being and moving my awareness beyond a singular view of me, and 'spiritual' as one very particular aspect of the transpersonal dimension. The transpersonal is not about belonging to a religious order of some kind or not belonging to a specific group or belief system. It is about belonging to myself and being able to honour and validate my own experiences of all those realms, other states of being, other ways of being that transport me beyond the 'normal' experiences of a single reality.

In 2006 I was a member of a small group undertaking a co-operative inquiry[10] (CI) into creating the conditions conducive to transpersonal

[10] Co-operative Inquiry is a rigorous and radical way of working in groups. It embodies the principles of individual personal responsibility, autonomy of action, peer relationships and paying attention to interpersonal issues (when they get in the way of the process), all as prior commitments to the purpose of the task of the inquiry itself. See *Co-operative Inquiry: Research into the Human Condition*, John Heron, Sage, 1996.

experiences. It was a fascinating and extremely illuminating process. I learned a great deal about how I enter into altered states – including discovering those strategies that are less effective for me, but which were effective for others. We unearthed a tremendous diversity of experience and understanding of even the terms themselves (i.e. transpersonal, spiritual) and we came to realise that our inquiry led to more questions than finding answers to already existing questions.

The key questions we began with were:

1. What qualifies as a 'genuine' transpersonal or spiritual experience?
2. How do you know if you have had one?

These are questions that have taxed countless people over the years; possibly ever since the concepts of transpersonal and spiritual were first consciously reflected upon. It is a valid and necessary exploration and such questions open up discussions about the whole area of the transpersonal and the spiritual.

The questioning, the shared experience, the willingness to be open to what comes and the willingness to experience a new way of entering altered states were all the journey in themselves. We only scratched the surface over those nine months yet I know I came away with an enriched sense of my own experiences and those of others. In addition, I gained a wonderful sense of how being together in a group with that kind of intent is both remarkable and incredibly powerful.

Universal Connections

As part of my exploration of altered states and my study of my patterns, I heard about the Archetypes that have been with us since the dawn of time. They are archetypal quite simply because they are found everywhere in all places and at all times, and they are reflected in themes that travel throughout all the ages in art, literature, music, myth and religion. Since they are archetypal, they live within us even though we might be unaware of them.

The Dao

In a very real sense, then, we are not separate beings but individuals within a greater collective. In touching this realm, my experience is that I do not lose my individual unique characteristics but become aware of a further dimension of being linked to all people in all times. The Tao (or Dao) holds the concept that we are all one; the Tao symbol stands for everything within and outside the cosmos – heaven and earth, nature and humanity, and all phenomena both known and yet undiscovered.

It is a very powerful and yet humbling experience to be part of all things and to feel no separation from them: another impetus for recognising that we are all equally valued, equally sacred and equally to be respected. The first time I experienced what I came to describe as a connection with all things I was overwhelmed, yet it is now a familiar, and joyous, feeling. That sense of connection has been deepened, expanded and, through this process, I was challenged to open my mind, my body, my spirit to even more possibilities.

Other Realms, Other Beings

There are beings – angels, spirit guides, elementals, animal guides[11], and allies – around me that 'visit' me: some of them are very positive; some are neutral; others I have experienced as being

[11] The nature of Animal Guides and how to discover your own guide is deeply rooted in a number of cultures and spiritual traditions, notably Native American and some South American peoples.

malignant. All manner of beings can be encountered within the limitless possibilities of altered states, the unconscious and the collective connection, and there are many practices that have ways of discovering and encountering them.

One very memorable experience for me was seeing a group of beings who I can only describe as being hubs. They were each at the centre of a wheel radiating from which were many spokes. They were the spirit callers. The spokes were other beings who they were guiding or drawing into the realm of working at the spirit level. There were five hubs: one felt like Buddha, one Jesus, one a woman on top of a mountain, one I couldn't identify and a fifth I came to know following a trip to China about a year later.

I reflected on these images for a long time and came to realise that they were not necessarily specific people but manifestations of energies; there was the Christ consciousness, the consciousness of the Buddha, the consciousness of the goddess – as I came to realise – and the fourth, a very hard thing to accept, was me. This was around the growing recognition that my 'work' is in these realms rather than on the physical plane; that this kind of work operates from a certain level of consciousness and that this was my potential.

I was welcomed by the four hubs as a long lost fellow spirit caller – something which felt very strange and awesome. And yet – it did fit with the experiences I was having and the kinds of work I was involved with in my guardian angel role and other, more wide-reaching, roles. I have come to view this as one of my closest networks.

The identity of the fifth hub came to light in 2004 when I travelled to China as part of a Tai Chi group following the Silk Road. It was an amazing trip with many memorable highlights but two stand out above all the rest. One revolved around a connection high in the mountains with one of my fellow travellers and the second centred on a Dongba Priest.

We were staying overnight in a wonderful small town – we rarely stayed anywhere more than one night on this trip! The people were friendly, open and delightful to be around. We were informed that we were to visit the local theatre for their performance that evening and our hearts sank; we had endured a number of such events most nights since arriving in the country almost three weeks earlier. So we went, fully intending to leave part way through and either go back to the hotel or wander around this really interesting, welcoming town.

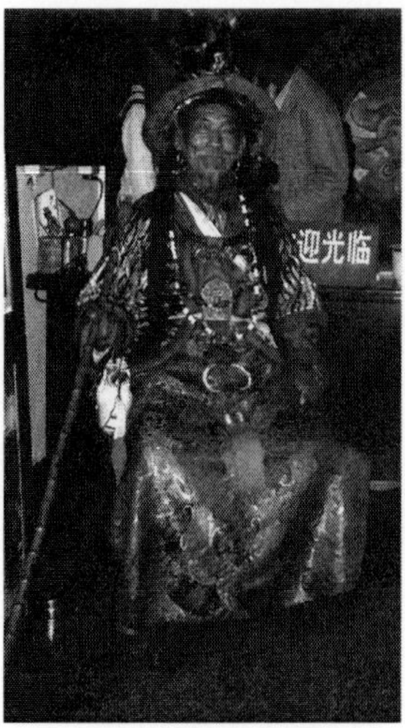

In the event, however, I was overawed, transfixed and transformed by the experience. In the entrance way to this small, beautiful theatre sat a man in the full regalia of his role; here was the Dongba chief priest. Our eyes met and we knew; we each knew the other from other realms. Here was the other 'hub'; that is how we knew each other. I was captivated by the twinkle in his eyes, the serenity he exuded and the stillness about him even though it was a hive of activity all around.

The connection between us continued even when he was on stage – finding and making eye contact amid the crowded audience. He is still with me in spirit realms and we meet frequently when we are working as a network; a wonderful example of spirit beings and beings still in human form working together and being recognisable to each other.

Not one of us wanted to leave this time and everyone in the group agreed that the performance was by far the best theatre visit of the whole trip. The performance was so real, so genuine and came from the heart of the local people and their own culture and beliefs. Yes, it was a performance for visitors but it was so much more than the other set pieces we had seen in the previous three weeks.

Guardian Angels

During a healing session on my jaw I had a visualisation of me as a young teenager where I was being hit by two men. In this scenario my parents didn't stop it; couldn't stop it. The sense is that everything that goes wrong in the house is my fault and the 'next-door neighbour' is the only one I can talk to about all this. His room is beautiful, safe, white and I could be there without fear, without terror, without being on 'red alert' all the time. It was clear to me that this was not some kind of repressed memory even though it was incredibly real, vivid and powerful. I knew it was acting as a metaphor and as a way of teaching me.

I knew that the neighbour was actually my Guardian Angel. The room and his presence were wonderful; slowly the walls became less solid and the room became more of an open space. It felt very much that this paralleled my process of letting go of old beliefs and becoming free; stepping out of the prison of my own pathology. In time, the room disappeared but I was still aware of his presence and could call on him and visit him at any time.

I was so grateful that I knew my Guardian Angel and valued his presence, the place of safety he offered me and the support he gave, yet the concept of the Guardian Angel didn't stay with me particularly strongly – until I visited Northumberland in 1998.

I was sitting high on the fellside with a wonderful view over the valley and an open grassy area where families were picnicking by the river. I could hear the muffled sounds of children playing and the general chatter of people having fun. It was a lovely still moment for me and then, suddenly, it was more. I could feel my presence over and around all the people down by the river. I could see and hear everything as clearly as if I was standing next to them. I had the vivid awareness that I was their Guardian Angel; my role to protect, support and be alongside.

It was one of those moments where I thought I was mad. Yet the feeling and the sense persisted and it was really clear that this, now, was also to be part of who I am and part of my service. Experiences of a similar nature began to occur regularly, always spontaneously – an important aspect for me since I could give them more credibility if they were unexpected and out of the blue. As is occasionally the case with me, as I learn more and have other experiences, a particular kind of awareness is, unconsciously, put to one side until something re-awakens it. And this is what happened with my Guardian Angel concept until...

In the summer of 2006, I had an appointment with my astrologer in Keswick and I was wondering what to do until it was time to meet him. I knew I didn't want to wander around the shops and I felt drawn to go down by the lake. What followed opened up a new stage in my journey.

Once by the lake, there was a strong, irresistible pull to walk along to Friar's Crag, so I followed the impulse. I perched on a rock for quite a while enjoying the view over the lake and to the fells beyond; cherishing the quiet, the stillness. Some people arrived but I felt no need to move. They stayed, talking loudly for some time, and then they moved on.

Next, a smaller, quieter group arrived and, this time, I felt I had to move on. I was about to head back into Keswick when I noticed the dog was wagging its tail frantically – its whole backend was going! So I turned back and was received rapturously by the dog. Those people moved off and I remained standing at the edge of the crag just looking out across the lake.

Then I became aware of a cloud of smoke and I felt irritated that someone was lighting a fire or something of that sort. I looked to see who was causing it and I saw that the younger woman of two who had been behind and to the side of me had released some ashes.

Initially I thought I ought to move in order to let them be private even though they must have known I was there because they would definitely be able to see me, yet my other sense was telling me very clearly to stay – to be a witness with them.

It really was moving – a privilege. The two women hugged and cried whilst the toddler with them clearly didn't understand what was happening. The younger woman took a photo of the older one (her mother?) I offered to take a photo of them both and then wished them all the best and went on my way.

I went down to the water's edge to paddle and then I saw the same women again. The older one came over and said that I had made the occasion for them. That it had made a tremendous difference; that they decided I must be an angel. I knew at that point it was her husband – I said, 'your husband'? 'Yes.' We had a lovely hug and she moved on after once again thanking me for making the occasion so special.

On reflection I knew that here was my reason for being drawn to the lake. Here was a further reminder to allow conditions to unfold; to trust the process. Here was another call to taking on this role as part of who I am. I now knew that the key component of all this is in presence; my presence for those two women on this occasion. It also felt like a challenge to step more fully into my role: to be less coy; less apologetic; less sceptical; to have less false modesty.

Where Now? Next Steps

Gradually, I became more willing and more enthusiastic about being taken on journeys by my spirit friends/guides and I became more familiar and less fearful of other experiences. I began to be able to 'see' more: where I was perhaps, or to recognise my purpose for being there, or know the person or group of people our presence was around. After many journeys, I was, in effect, given my 'wings' in a wonderfully moving and powerful experience, and I began 'travelling' on my own and taking others on their first journeys.

This is when I really began to have a greater sense of what it would mean to grow into 'become who you were born to be'. This is why I had needed to give up work in the conventional sense of the word. This is why I had had to slow down, to stop. I had to stop and radically re-assess my life, let go of so much, struggle with my identity, my sense of self-worth, how I viewed my value to society and more, all in order to have the space, the energy, the growing stillness, the time to commit to this true 'work' – though it never feels like work in the sense of toil or labour or other feelings often attributed to employment.

As these kinds of experiences became more frequent, still often unsought and unexpected, I began to accept that there was indeed something mysterious and wonderful happening. I had the capacity to be in touch with things far beyond myself. I had the capacity to tap into a collective awareness, a fundamental level of knowledge and understanding about realities, connectedness, the existence of beings in a way that our society generally either is completely unaware of or chooses to deny.

I realised that all my experiences could, if I let them, be a way in which I separated myself from most other people in my world. After all, most people are not having these kinds of experiences. Further, as these experiences and my growing understanding take me deeper into my journey, other realms and what this means for how I choose to live my life, there are fewer and fewer people with whom it is possible to share them. There are, therefore, major implications for how I live my life and how I continue to be in a world that, by and large, is not aware of these possibilities. The crux, then, is how to live the transformations I experience, and this is the focus of the next chapter.

6

Being in the World

Introduction

A challenging moment came when I knew with absolute certainty that this is not a hobby; it is not an 'add-on' to my life – it is my life. It is my true path; it is my destiny. It is the very essence of my being that always needs priority and, as such, must have my full attention with mindfulness.

I know with certainty that I am called to live my journey in the world – not separate to or segregated from the world. Everything I have experienced, everything I have learned, every insight, every painful moment of facing my inner darkness will show itself in some way in my life and will be seen in some form or another by all those around me. Inevitably, therefore, there are consequences and implications for my way of life, my world, my relationships, my self-image, my everyday life.

Some of these consequences have been wonderful, liberating, joyous and – to quote a friend recently – lead to feeling 'fucking brilliant'; some have given rise to distress, uncertainty and challenge. Part of my learning in this process included being able to accept all consequences 'as the imposters they are' (to distort the famous poem). I learned to recognise and accept that things are as they are and then to look at where that takes me as I find my new way of being in the world.

This chapter, therefore, explores the ways in which all the work that has gone before informs how I operate, what I choose as my priorities, and something of the demands, challenges, implications and consequences I faced as I sought to bring my new Self, my transformed Self, into the world.

Living the Transformation

I have described some of my experiences as being 'beyond my imagination' and that is exactly what they have felt like, whilst others have formed part of extended conscious work to shift a pattern, for example. However they are experienced, they have that element of challenging me to be different, to see the world differently, to *live in the world differently.*

From the very beginning of my awakening, a question that was always with me was, 'Is this a permanent transformation or a temporary high spot which will go away?' It led me to wondering how I would know when a transformation had taken place and what that would mean. I now believe that a transformation has taken place when I experience a fundamental difference in the way I view the world or how I view myself in my world. It is so much more than change and development, and yet it encompasses both.

> "Transformation…incorporates development and includes change. Transformation results in a qualitative shift in state, function and processes involved. A new order of operating comes into play. A new mode of functioning appears. The previous way of operating is not simply replaced but superseded and transcended. The old functions are not necessarily abandoned, but others are introduced that exceed previous limitations. Processes are integrated into a higher order of functioning."
>
> **Bryce Taylor,** *Helping People Change,* pp4-5. Oasis Press, 1995.

All the many changes and shifts and transformations I have been through affect every single aspect of my life. A change of friends; a change of occupation; a change of priorities; a change in how I perceive my place in the world; a change in how I see myself and my own worth; a change in how I relate to others; a change in what I choose to be associated with. It has been really difficult at times to know when to let go of an old way of being; to know when it has outstayed its welcome as it were – when it is past its 'sell-by-date'. Taking that step into a different way of operating can be difficult; timing is important, support is critical.

Naturally, all this impinges on those around me. Some people left because it was difficult for them to hear and be with me in my new and different world. With others, we began to have less and less in common, and so we gently drifted apart. When I stepped out of the church one of the consequences was that almost all of the relationships I thought would stand the transition did not do so.

My transformations have a number of characteristics. Some, for example, were primarily apparent only to me since they were part of my inner journey, whilst others have been much more evident in my wider world, such as the way in which I operate in groups.

In addition, although I may experience a transformation primarily as an inner shift, it is inevitable that such an inner transformation will manifest itself in the world as it becomes more and more integrated within me.

I have had sudden and immediately life-changing 'light bulb' moments, whereas other experiences that appeared to arrive 'out of the blue' were actually the outcome of much work and commitment. Yet others gradually became integrated, and I only became consciously aware of them when I realised that I was behaving differently, feeling differently or having a new response to a familiar situation.

In 2006, a metaphor came to me that goes some way to describing how I feel about all that has happened and how my place in the world, the roles I play and the calling I feel have been truly transformed. I had the image of an orchestral concert and the differing parts people have, all of which are important to the whole. I could see how I had been in each position in this scenario during my journey and it was remarkable to see the development in this way.

Since writing the piece opposite, I have become aware of yet another step within this metaphor, that of enabling 'conductors' to step into their role, a hugely significant shift in my understanding of my own role.

The Orchestra

Outsider: *not knowing there is anything happening; being on the edge and not believing I belonged*

↓

Bystander: *outside the concert hall, knowing there is something inside that others value; not knowing how to be involved, not wanting to be involved, or both*

↓

Audience member: *listening to the music*

↓

Participant: *feeling the music, being affected by it*

↓

Player: *a member of the orchestra; making the music*

↓

Solo performer: *in addition to being a general member of the orchestra; making my music*

↓

Conductor: *orchestrating the music, enabling all to make our music whilst still having the capacity to be a solo performer*

Heather Tweddle

Living with the Unexpected

I increasingly recognised that I needed to be willing to suspend my rational/logical thoughts and beliefs but it took me longer to act upon it. There is little space for the logic and rigid structure of society in the realms of the universe and of the cosmos, but I didn't always find it easy to suspend my judgements about what is and is not possible. This is an integral part of accepting that I have no way of knowing – nor would I choose to, now – where my journey will lead me or what I might experience. What I did know was that I would be changed by my experiences, though quite how an experience, or a breakthrough in transcending distorted behaviours, or an insight, would manifest itself in my life was often a mystery.

I was initially fearful of the unexpected: Would I manage? Would I cope? What would happen? Living with a degree of constant unknowing and the unexpected was hard for me until a number of experiences transformed the anxiety into a sense of wonder, expectation, anticipation and an awareness of witnessing my life.

Expectancy and anticipation are connected to a sense of awe, of the child-like capacity to gaze around the world with inquiring eyes, mind and spirit. Expectancy becomes the capacity to see anew each day. It becomes the state where I am touched by the wonder of the Universe; it becomes the place where I enter each moment with an unattached anticipation of what my journey might bring. I discovered that a good place from which to operate is to expect the unexpected all the time.

I was driving around South Island, New Zealand, a few years ago and it is no exaggeration to say that every corner, every brow of a hill, every change of direction brought new, amazing views. I realised after a while that I was anticipating every corner and the

top of each pass with the excitement of a child opening Christmas or birthday presents.

It was truly exhilarating and was made more so by realising that this is how I can approach my spiritual travels too. I was struck by the awareness that this sense of expectancy of what might appear did not detract from what I was currently experiencing; it was a balance of the two.

Further, I came to understand in a very different and living way the connection between past and future fulfilled in the moment. At times, the views in my rear or wing mirrors were equally stunning. I had a tremendously clear view of where I had come from, but from a different perspective. Equally, I had a clear view, on occasions, of the road ahead yet I was very much in the present – at that spot on the road at that moment in my life. The past informing, the future beckoning and both being lived now.

This led me to an awareness of *emergence*; allowing what will to emerge with a sense of expectancy, openness and flexibility. Emergence is a process of 'sitting with' a theme, a situation, intent, or simply sitting in openness, and it cannot be forced. I found that if I attempt to control what will happen, what will appear, what will manifest itself, then the process is not free, is not open and is not conducive to emergence. Emergence, therefore, is more likely to occur the more I am able to let go of specific, controlled outcomes.

Having Intent

Yi-Intent

Intent in this context and sense is very closely linked to emergence and to letting go of outcomes. Intent is less restricting and rigid than having a definitive object that I am searching for or which I am expecting. It is more about a mind-set, an approach to whatever experience is being undertaken. So, for example, my intent might be to find those conditions that enable me more easily to enter altered states. Or, I might have the intent to notice what happens and how it influences my state. I might have intent to simply sit with the state and see where it takes me. I might focus upon a particular theme, being open to discover what emerges. I may 'hold' a person for healing. The crucial difference is that there is flexibility and spaciousness for the divine to enter in, for the presence of grace, for the numinous to live and be experienced within.

I encountered a wonderful example of the power of intent in the Sri Mariamman Hindu Temple in Singapore[12], in February 2002. Shortly after arriving it became clear there was to be a prayer

[12] The Sri Mariamman Temple is the oldest Hindu temple in Singapore. Built in 1827, Mariamman Kovil or Kling Street Temple as it was popularly known then, was constructed for worship by immigrants from the Nagapatnam and Cuddalore districts of South India. The temple is dedicated to Goddess Mariamman, known for her power in curing epidemic illnesses and diseases.

service. I asked if I could stay to watch. 'Yes,' came the reply. So I sat down on the floor facing up the temple. It was truly amazing. There was lots of drumming and other musical instruments playing; a cacophony yet it all created harmony too. I had none of my usual desire to put my hands over my ears when there is loud music or noise; I simply sank into the rhythms and the sounds.

A door opened in front of the main shrine – beautiful beyond description – and a priest entered the central part of the temple. He performed various rituals including lighting flames and receiving gifts from those present. There was a lot of what appeared to be random moving around involving three shrines; seemingly informal yet obviously deeply important.

I felt so connected to it and caught up in it, and I was in what I would now call a deeply altered state. I felt really at ease – there was peace and such a sense of belonging too. I didn't want to move at the end.

As I reluctantly stood up to go, the man I had asked if I could stay came to me and asked if I would like to receive some of the blessed rice yoghurt. 'YES.' I did hesitate but only because I knew 'outsiders' were not normally admitted. I asked if it was OK and it was. So I followed him into the main part of the temple, which is permanently roped off and inaccessible to tourists. I was given the rice yoghurt by one of the priests and I stood there with the worshippers; some looked at me but I felt nothing from them other than an overwhelming sense of acceptance, alongside an understandable curiosity and interest.

A few other tourists tried to come into the temple part and they were turned back. The way they looked at me was very interesting! As I moved away – somewhat reluctantly since I did not want this to end – I realised that **it's not the religion or the rituals that matter; it is the intention that is crucial.** There was a shared sense of something greater, wider, higher; that is what was important.

I felt awed and hugely privileged to be accepted into their worshipping community in this way. I had felt the atmosphere as soon as I had entered the complex: it felt electric; it felt so easy; I felt at home. It was this inner response that gave rise to the desire to stay for the prayer service whilst the other tourists moved on as it began.

I'm sure the man saw/felt something in me far beyond that of a tourist. That he, too, had made the connection that it is intention and awareness that is important and not a creed or religion or any particular ritual. This experience set me up for my whole trip! It certainly shifted some of my attitudes and helped me to lower barriers and move beyond patterns. It was truly transformational and amazing.

My intent to be with myself, the universe and the Divine, is one way in which I open myself up to so much more; it is a crucial dimension of my quest. My intent to allow what will happen to happen is freeing and liberating. The willingness to be with myself, together with the willingness and the intent to go with whatever might be, forms a major part of surrendering to the process, to the Divine.

Living a Life with Indifference

One major factor in discovering how I would bring my journey into the world was in developing indifference. When the word 'indifference' was first used in a conversation with me, my initial reaction was that the other person wasn't interested or, worse, didn't care. It has taken me a while, but I now understand and realise it is as far removed from those two fears as it can be. Indifference is the state of being unattached to outcomes, to relationships even, to any particular experience or feeling, and this form of detachment (the witness) is an essential feature of stepping into the unknown and all aspects of the spiritual life.

When I am indifferent (not uninterested) to any given experiences or feelings that I meet on my journey, I am more able to see them and experience them for what they truly are. I am, in turn, less likely to invest them with my own 'baggage', my own unaddressed issues and patterns – or even any addressed ones that are still hanging around! There will, therefore, be less getting in the way of a real, genuine, congruent response both to my own needs and to those of others.

Being non-attached, to a possession, say, or an idea, or the way a particular part of my journey will work out, is another facet of indifference. Letting go of needing to have complete answers about where I might end up, and even any idea of the impact or consequences before stepping out, is part of the work of the warrior. Also, if I cling to what I hold as outcomes I am preventing myself from experiencing the full potential of what might occur. Sitting with expectancy is one thing; sitting with the expectancy that *this* will happen is something else and will close down the process.

If I can enter any situation with no attachment to how it is going to end then I will be able to respond much more freely whilst in the situation. I will be more flexible, more willing to shift a position and bring more presence to the whole picture rather than my own 'pet' stance and what I want to happen/get/achieve.

This concept of indifference is also important and relevant when considering other people's journeys. This is not to say that I am uninterested in someone else's experiences, far from it, but understanding the concept has enabled me to let go of needing someone to be a particular way, behave in a certain way or respond in a way I want. I become unattached to how they respond to me and I am not caught up in their being any way other than how they are.

This can be difficult, especially if the other 'pushes my buttons' in some way or if I have a sense of their next step, which they are unable to take on at that moment. However, when achieved, indifference and disinterest means that I am able to be with the other person in whatever state they find themselves, laying no expectations on them – or myself. Cultivating indifference of this quality allows what needs to happen to happen without restricting or confining the person[13] or what can take place.

[13] Naturally, there needs to be clear contracting between the people concerned as to the limits of what is dealt with in any healing session and what is taken elsewhere – to counselling perhaps.

Therefore, in being indifferent to the other's experience, I allow them their freedom to take their own path, make their own decisions and take responsibility for this. There is true wonder in seeing someone unfold and grow into their own way of being; there is true joy in travelling along with someone in their journey. This is a supportive and enabling role and does not take any of the individual's personal power away from them.

At this level of indifference, there is no ego getting in the way and there are no dangerous comparisons being made. There is a danger, for example, of believing that if I have not had the same experience as him, say, then somehow my journey is lesser than. Or, that if I have had a particular experience, insight or whatever, to believe that I am further along the road than her, say. Nothing could be further from the reality of the situation. If I am focussing on comparing my journey with someone else's then I am not fully engaged in my own, and there is no place for envy or jealousy of another's journey. My journey is mine. Your journey is yours. We may travel similar paths; we may have complementary experiences yet our journeys truly are unique. None is better or right, and none is worse or wrong. We have freedom to make our own choices and responsibility to take for our own journey at whatever level is right for us at a given time. Authenticity (or congruence) and genuineness are the only 'standards'.

My journey is about returning, re-discovering my true, my inherent nature, and to do this I need to develop indifference in the sense described here. When I achieve this, I free myself from spending energy worrying what others might think if I do this or say that; I free myself from taking responsibility for how others might respond to me as a consequence of how I am; I free myself from the need to 'second guess' what the other is thinking, needing.

Discovering this indifference thus enhances my capacity for giving my full attention to my journey; doing what I need to do whilst allowing others to do what they need to do. I increased my understanding of this whilst on the magical island of Iona.

The Beauty of Rocks and Sea

I am sitting on top of a rugged outcrop of rocks by the sea
The sea is not particularly rough but it is still pounding the rocks; spray bouncing high into the air

I can feel the vibration of the battering the rocks are receiving
In an instant I am aware of both sea and rocks
I am part of both

The sea is doing what it does; the rocks are doing what they do

There is no resentment of the rocks towards the sea for the damage in the way of erosion – this is simply how it is

No desire on the part of the sea to undermine or damage the rocks; it simply is as it is

Each is fulfilling its true nature and its role in creation
Each is accepting of what is done and what they do

Heather Tweddle

The rocks and the sea on Iona and their indifference to the outcome of their actions also gave me new insight into the concept of *surrendering* to my journey. Until that moment, I believed that surrender meant losing control or giving up yet I came to realise this is far from how it is. Surrender is a positive and pro-active decision to embrace more of… Surrendering is about *accepting my full potential* and letting go of preconceived ideas of what that might mean. It is about surrendering to what I know to be my true path, my 'bliss', with dedication, commitment and living a life with indifference.

Communication in my Wider World

One of the key elements of living *my* journey, living *my* transformations, living the experiences and insights I gain, is that of communicating with others. These 'others' include my family, friends and acquaintances, all of whom can be rather perplexed by changes they see in my life and in my way of being. They also include fellow travellers, with whom it is a joy to be able to share experiences freely, and beings from other realities. Whoever and wherever they are, communication is important.

As I am more able to transcend my compulsive behaviours, the more free I am to relate to others and to 'be' in the world, and this will be noticed and felt by others, often without any words. Huge signals are given out by the way we hold ourselves physically; by those things to which we choose to pay attention; by how we relate to the world around us; by how we relate to the people around us. This can lead to people feeling threatened by what they see as a new person developing; not the one they married, say, or not the one with whom they have been working for years.

Having said this, oral language is hugely important too, yet even people who feel they are on similar journeys can have difficulties in communicating to each other such personal and unique experiences. The language we have is not always adequate to convey a felt experience or a sense of something beyond our current understanding even to ourselves, let alone other people.

I am learning to experience beyond the norms of society; I am learning to be more open to the unexpected, to the 'impossible' and, as a consequence, frequently I search with difficulty for words to describe what is happening and what I am feeling. It is as though I need to learn a new language.

Even when I could find words that were good enough, I didn't really know what I wanted to talk about, or how much, or to whom.

To Talk or not to Talk

Do I wish to communicate anything to anyone else?

If so, who?

Why do I feel the need to share my journey?

Do I need to share anything?

If I do, which parts will I share?

How much will I share?

Who will I share what with?

Can I find the words to describe my experiences?

What consequences might there be if I do talk about my journey?

Heather Tweddle

These questions enabled me to explore more about how I wish to manage my experiences around others, as well as taking me further into my own process. Reflecting upon them helped illuminate what role I truly wished others to play – or not – and highlighted those ego remnants that I still had around me.

Early on in my journey, I had two very contrasting examples of the consequences of talking freely. One, my then parish priest, was amazing. He truly heard everything I said; he listened to my struggles; he affirmed my place in those struggles; he talked freely of his own stance. He played a hugely significant role as I began to discover what I believed for myself and began to see that this was not, actually, 'heretical'.

The other, a very close friend of over six years, said she could no longer have such conversations with me because they were undermining her faith and they were threatening. However, it was not simply 'those' conversations that stopped; she ended the relationship completely. It was very abrupt and extremely painful for me, especially since I had felt I was part of her whole family, sharing many family meals and watching with pleasure as her two young children grew and developed.

On the first occasion I shared one of my experiences around Christ and our mutual and equal sacredness with a small group of my fellow Readers, people I thought I knew well, they described my experiences and my understanding as heretical (which, of course, it is in the traditional Christian Church). It certainly felt risky to talk about it but I had not anticipated the strength of response. I was shaken by it and, later, I realised I was angry too, because I felt that they had tried to take away the validity of my own experience, which I was only just beginning to trust. I can now recognise that their response was less about 'trashing' my experience and more about them feeling threatened in their own fairly rigid positions. This was another marker on my way to stepping beyond the formal, traditional Church.

For me, therefore, there have always been questions concerning how much I say of what experiences to whom. My sense of discernment and selectivity has developed over the years and I now have different places where I talk of different parts of my life. I actively seek people who can truly hear what I say, even though they might not understand; discovering safe places to speak my truth in a way that feels right for me. This kind of forum is a wonderful and vital part of living and developing my practice.

The Healing Arena

Healing has been an integral and important part of my spiritual journey in many ways. In addition to prearranged meetings where healing was on the agenda, I have received healing by simply being in the presence of supportive others. These experiences resulted in healing at every level – spiritual, emotional, psychological and physical – just like the ripples affecting and encompassing a whole pond. It was when I first asked Bryce how he approached this kind of healing that I was introduced to the concept of intent.

It was not that he had a specific thought in mind, more that he was using his energy to enable mine to begin to do what it needed to do. And, of course, this does not always mean an instant miraculous cure. Since healing of the body is so closely linked with healing of mind and soul, it is very often the case that healing of the body is slower in order to allow all the processes to come together. Healing of this nature can raise all manner of issues that may have lain buried for many years and which, only now, can be surfaced and worked with.

As I learned more, there was a shift in my process when I realised that I had the capacity to be with others in their journey: to hear their stories; to hear their experiences and be with them in their struggles. I began to ask myself whether I wanted to become involved in healing in some formal way. If so, how would this manifest itself? Did I wish to become a practitioner of some kind and offer my services to others? Would I undertake formal training in a recognised system such as Reiki[14] or shamanic practices or some form of physical therapy? Or would I prefer to follow my own journey and work with those who find their way to me organically as part of my service?

In any sphere of life it is inevitable to meet the modern phenomena of qualifications and accreditation. I soon met this in my spiritual journey through such activities as training to become a therapeutic massage practitioner, healing courses, and shamanic workshops. Therefore, when I was contemplating whether to become a formal healing practitioner of some kind I had to consider where I stood in connection with qualifications and accreditation.

Modern life is very goal oriented and outcomes and results seem to be the current 'gods' by which value is given to a group, organisation or individual. There are so many areas of life in our society where there is this on-going drive for acquiring more qualifications and much greater accreditation yet where do issues of validity, qualifications, assessment and accreditation fit in the spiritual journey?

Formal qualifications would be completely contra to the notion of taking up my own journey, though, naturally, formal accreditation may be desirable for those who wish to practice their particular discipline with others. The distinction, to me, seems to lie in the intent behind seeking qualifications. If there is a sense of needing to have qualifications, 'bits of paper', for the sake of having them then it would suggest that this has become more important than the journey itself. On the other hand, seeking further experiences, further insights that might lead organically

[14] Reiki is a Japanese technique for stress reduction and relaxation that also promotes healing. It is administered by 'laying on hands' and is based on the idea that an unseen life force energy flows through us and is what causes us to be alive.

to some kind of formal acknowledgement is *informing* the journey rather than *driving* the journey.

I see *accountability* as being hugely important, but this is very different from a culture of increasingly demanding accreditation and paper qualifications, which seems inappropriate to my personal and spiritual journey. I therefore chose not to go down the route of acquiring such qualifications, which raised the issue of whether a self-accountable approach is sufficient to avoid the dangers of a self-referential journey – grandiosity, delusion, illusion. This is something upon which I reflect at regular intervals yet having made huge shifts in valuing and accepting the primacy of my own experience, it seems only natural that I also have primacy over my own accountability.

Although my path is largely solitary, this does not necessarily mean a path in isolation from others. I meet with others of like-mind and I have a group of people who I consider to be my support group with regard to my journey; I believe this is essential to counter-balance my solitary path. It is in places like this where I ask for and receive feedback concerning how others see the authenticity and congruence of my journey.

An environment that is supportive and yet rigorous, where each person feels safe enough to share what they wish of their journeys, is an excellent forum for exploring the whole dimension of the spiritual path and growing levels of consciousness and awareness. The idea of co-creation in this kind of forum is an exciting one and one which, for me, holds the way for the future: it is an incredibly healing space in its own right.

Integrating the Learning

Information overload can be a very real consequence of this work unless time is given to absorbing and integrating the new, the bizarre, the unimaginable. There is a very definite difference between being in the midst of a seemingly continuous flow of experiences – as has happened at certain stages in my journey – and deliberately searching out new, ever more intense or varied experiences at the expense of taking time to reflect, integrate, assimilate and *live* what is already present.

The important shift in focus for me came when I realised that having all these new and exciting experiences was amazing but if I did not live them, if I did not integrate them in some way into my being, then I would become an experience 'junkie' rather than a seeker or a spiritual warrior.

Integration is more than simply being aware that I have these separate aspects within me and it is even more than being able to function well in each of them; it is the capacity to experience all of them – possibly simultaneously – and being able to move seamlessly between them as appropriate. Living out of my psychological being, for example, does not mean that I have switched off other aspects, such as my spiritual, physical or sexual dimensions. It is about appropriateness for the circumstances and the moment more than having to choose one to the exclusion of the others. This does not mean either, of course, that there have to be 'special' times and places for our spiritual being to be present.

Commitment to the Journey

Discipline is an unpopular word in many ways these days yet I believe it is important for me to maintain a discipline with regard to my spiritual practice.

> "An essential part of discipline is the development of an awareness of our responsibility and power of choice. The capacity of awareness we assign to that portion of the mind we call conscious or consciousness. We are now at the point where we can define spiritual growth as the growth or evolution of consciousness."
> **M Scott Peck,** *The Road Less Travelled,* p300. Arrow, 1990.

In the Concise Oxford Dictionary, discipline is defined as "bringing under control; punishing; training to obedience", however it also defines it as a "branch of learning". Discipline, in the sense I am using it here, is linked very closely with commitment; commitment to myself and commitment to the work that is my life (a "branch of learning"). And it is *self*-imposed; it is not punitive, it is not judgemental and it is not externally focussed.

The impetus for this work and the commitment to creating the optimum conditions for my own growth needs to come from within me. Being told to do something might work for some people and may be a wake-up call, a jumping off place, but for a continuing and growing development, the desire and the discipline have to come from within.

Anyone who has tried to give up smoking, for example, is likely to know this more than others. Being told something is 'bad for you' is not a sufficient motive to stop doing whatever 'it' is until I decide for myself and I am committed to the course of action. Only then is it likely that any prolonged and lasting change will occur. (This is equally true, of course, when being told something is 'good for you' and therefore you 'should' do it.)

My journey demanded commitment and a willingness to be disciplined, yet I also became aware that I could let discipline become a tyrannous force. Discipline can lead to an inflexible and rigid stance to the work, which, in turn, can lead to a lack of spontaneity and joy in the unexpected. It can also lead to, 'I must do… because I said I would'. This is a relatively trivial example perhaps, but one to which I was prone and which needed considerable attention before I moved beyond it. I need to have flexibility and an alertness to my inner wisdom, to prevent discipline becoming a driven response that then undermines all I am undertaking. It was with all this in mind that my practice began to evolve and unfold quite organically.

> "Even the simplest of pleasures is a craft, a discipline that demands time and effort."
>
> **Zaleski & Kaufman,** *Gifts of the Spirit,* p87. HarperSanFrancisco, 1998.

7

Inspirations and Influences

Introduction

From the very first feeling that something was missing in my life right up to the time of writing this book, I have been influenced by and have learned a great deal from a wide range of people, events, strategies and approaches to spirituality. Without them my journey would be less rich, less alive, less real and would not have evolved as organically as it has.

The greatest impact upon me has been the people who have travelled with me for varying lengths of time. They have been – and remain – particularly vital and instrumental in enabling me to be where I am and, because their contributions are so important and so pivotal to my survival and to my transformation, I have dedicated the final chapter to the people in my journey.

This chapter, however, describes other forms of inspiration and influence; highlighting their significance and the impact they have had on me and my developing practice. These stimuli and catalysts, unexpected and expected, appeared from many quarters: from life experiences, from life transitions, from various forms of Divination tools, from strategies, from activities. Some have been transient whilst others are continually influential and important; some were key to my awakening, whilst others came along later. Within this diversity, the common theme was the need for me to remain awake to possibilities and not close down or ignore what appear to be unlikely events as teachers or unlikely people as angels.

Figure 2 opposite gives an overview of these significant influences, in no particular order. Those in ordinary font are expanded upon further in this chapter whilst the four dimensions that have been consistently and continually of prime importance (which are given considerable prominence elsewhere in the book), i.e. people, meditation, spirit guides and allies, non-ordinary experiences and altered states, are in bold.

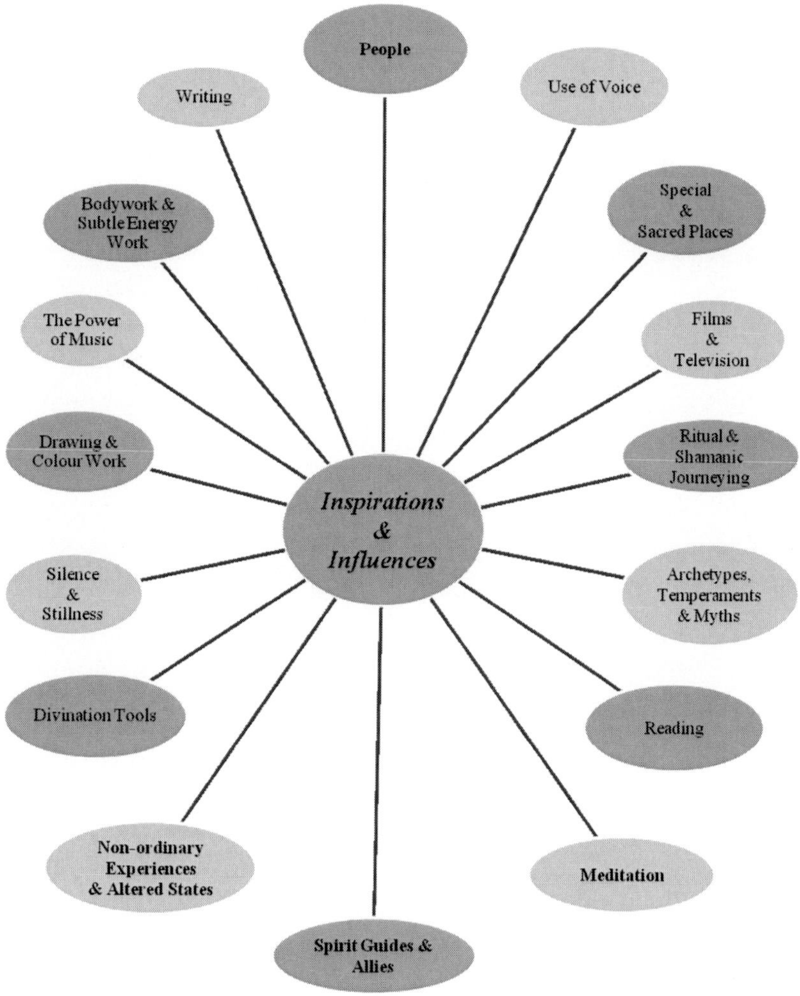

Figure 2: Inspirations and Influences

Writing

In the early days, I just could not talk openly and freely about how I was feeling, about what was going on in my deepest being or express such negative (as I viewed them then) emotions as anger, hate, envy and jealousy. I felt as though I would explode with all that was held inside; like a pressure cooker with no release valve. I was encouraged first by Paul ('my' CPN) and then by Bryce to write about what was going on, and I found a whole new world opening to me.

Sometimes there would only be about ten words on a page because the writing was so large and violent. The anger, the fear and all manner of feelings poured out of me onto the page like water pouring from a bursting dam. It was a non-edited, non-intellectual 'splurge'. Such anger, such rage and such fear found a place yet there were also times when I couldn't even write and simply scribbled so hard the pen ripped through the paper. On these occasions it was like looking at the paper through a burning red haze with the eyes of a completely different person; someone who was not the 'nice' person she had always hoped she was but someone with strong, so far unspoken, needs and feelings.

I discovered that I could write freely – there was no editing of what I said because it was for my eyes only. I had so much fear of what others might think if they heard more about the 'real' me, so it was much easier to write these 'unspeakable' things down for them to read rather than say it to them. After a time, I found it incredibly helpful to be able to send what I had written to Paul or Bryce, and it proved a good 'entry point' into a session. This was an enormous time of release and was a major contributory factor in reducing my inner fury and the desire to hurt myself.

In addition to this release, writing helped to stop the endless cycles in my head where I would go over and over the same thing:

obsessing; getting stuck in a rut in my fears and my thinking. This, in turn, enabled me to begin to break free from all the self-defeating constant inner chatter. When I wrote without any planning or without even thinking about what I was going to say, I found that it freed me to take the next step in understanding or simply to let go a bit more of what was holding me.

Writing has been of great value to me when exploring difficult issues, concepts, and events. So, for example, when I was enduring terrific levels of pain in my joints at the time of the CFS diagnosis, I wrote to the pain. This process enabled me to learn more about how I related to myself as someone in constant pain and to find ways in which I could help myself.

Creative story making is another way in which writing enabled me to explore and understand more of myself. As I allowed my inner Self to do the writing/telling of the story, I could explore the characters, metaphors and images that arose in my writing and learn a great deal about my life: what I needed; what I wanted; how come I behaved in a certain way and much more. Setting to one side my more rational, logical thought processes and allowing the creative through was a gateway to an amazing new world.

> "If the experience of 'cosmic consciousness' is unspeakable, it is true that in trying to utter it in words one is not saying anything in the sense of conveying information or making a proposition. The speech expressing such an experience is more like an explanation. Or better, it is the speech of poetry rather than logic, though not poetry in the impoverished sense of the logical positivist, the sense of decorative and beautiful nonsense."
>
> **Alan Watts,** *This Is It,* p20. Rider, 1960.

There came a time when I realised my writing was serving another purpose too. There was less need for it to be an escape or a release from the unspoken and frightening, and it was now about recognising how it brought the unconscious to my conscious awareness. This led me to writing more creatively about many of my transpersonal and altered reality experiences, some of which are included in this book. Writing continues to be a major part of my journey and my practice.

Use of Voice

Words, of course, are equally powerful when spoken and they can be a form of meditation in themselves, such as toning[15] or mantras.

> "The etymological root of 'mantra' is man, Sanskrit for 'to think', and to say a mantra thus implies conscious pondering rather than mindless trancelike bliss. Nonetheless, a mantra's real power lies in the miraculous nature of the sound itself, a chord in the song of the absolute, uncreated cosmos."
>
> **Zaleski & Kaufman,** *Gifts of the Spirit,* p111. HarperSanFrancisco, 1998.

In July 1994 I attended a one-day healing workshop led by Matthew Manning and Tim Wheater. Tim's music was amazing: it was magical and mystical; the sounds, the tones and the way he led us through a series of Ohms were awesome and amazingly liberating. This was the first inkling I had that I have the capacity to tone for an incredibly long time without needing to breathe in

[15] Toning is the creation of extended vocal sounds on a single vowel in order to experience the sound and its effects in other parts of the body. The repeated toning of vowels creates a reverberation so that when the chanting stops, the sounds continue to echo within the mind and within the chambers of the body. A particular vibration resonates with the vibrational quality of the energy centres of the body in a way that enables the body to balance its natural energies thus leading to healing.

the conventional sense and that I can heal through toning. The feedback I received at the end of the workshop about the heat and energy in my hands and the impact of my toning supported my growing belief in my capacity to heal.

Further, this experience contributed hugely to being more in touch with my inner creativity: an area I'd previously believed pretty much didn't exist. I had the belief that I couldn't sing – or not in tune anyway – I couldn't dance, I certainly couldn't heal (what, little ol' me!). It has taken many years and lots of events, experiences, and patient people, before I was able to own and acknowledge that this is something which is natural for me.

Ohm: Birth, Death, Life

I began a Yoga class in 2009, primarily to keep me physically more flexible, to develop more stamina and generally tone my muscles, but what I didn't know was that each class ends with us all chanting three Ohms[16]. We have also used different sounds to connect specifically with each energy centre (chakra); a very powerful healing experience and a welcome re-connection to using my voice in this way.

Over the years, I know there has been a clear connection between finding my voice through toning, chanting and such like, and becoming increasingly free in expressing more of who I am, owning my journey, being able to speak my truth.

[16] Ohm is a Hindu sacred sound, called 'the mother of all mantras', and is said to have been the first word ever spoken. It represents the universal events of birth and death and, even more, life; it is at the centre of everything. Some also say that the four parts (birth, life, death, the whole) symbolise four stages of consciousness: awake, sleeping, dreaming, and a trance or transcendental state.

Bodywork and Subtle Energy Work

I place a tremendous importance upon the bodywork I have received from a number of people using different approaches. Healing I received on my body – my jaw, shoulder and neck in particular – led to a tremendous release of emotion and to insights into my journey. Further, the revelations through the massage I received opened my eyes to a whole new world – or worlds. It was the same massage practitioner with whom I had the experience of swimming with dolphins in their environment who saw the potential in me for healing, for hands-on work. She suggested I work on her; a way forward that would never have crossed my mind without her intervention.

The concept of body memories was a new one to me and as my journey continues I become increasingly convinced of the power of memories held within my body. This is not just for this life either. Yes, I had ignored injuries and, yes, I had not honoured the seriousness of spinal surgery but it goes even deeper and further than this. Links with pre-verbal stages, with pre-birth and past life experiences are held in the body, all of which can be accessed, worked with and processed in such a way as to enable greater understanding of myself and how come I am the way I am in the world. This, in turn, gives rise to opportunities to change these ways, if I choose to.

This, for me, is an integral part of the spiritual path. It is not only about integration either, the memories – often painful – influence and colour how I view the world, how I live in the world, how I relate to myself and to others. Addressing such deep body memories has been crucial for me in becoming free from my automatic responses – my default position – that so often did not give me the response I was looking for.

There have been two or three practitioners from whom I felt it was inappropriate to receive body or energy work, and learning to trust my intuition, my instinct, took some time but it was really important to do so. Interestingly, it is only recently that I felt at ease with receiving such work from other women (apart from a key contribution from Maggie, which I describe in *Healing through Meeting*). The shift took place during and following a shamanic journey I undertook in 2008 whilst on one of my Rievaulx retreats. It focussed on my transition from 'Mother' to 'Crone'[17], with much of what appeared being connected to female energy and the sense of allowing that part of me to become more accessible and free as part of stepping into the role of the Crone.

It has been vital to learn how to filter energy and be discriminatory about what I allow in. This is not to say I avoid certain people, more that I can now recognise what is appropriate for me at any given moment and in any particular situation. If there appears to be a difficulty with one person or persons, then it is the time to explore that, not necessarily with them, so that I can become aware of how that relationship works – or not – and become free within it. It is part of my growing sense of self-worth and discernment to recognise that I do not have to accept bodywork or energy work from someone just because they offer it.

[17] Although I have not given birth to children, I knew I needed to explore how the archetype and concept of Mother as the creative, life-giving force has been present in my life. In recognising and celebrating this I was then able to begin the transition into the next phase of the Crone – the Elder, the Wise Woman. I know the call to this exploration was partly my chronological age (I had reached 60 a few months earlier) yet it felt even more related to the stage I had reached in my journey.

Special and Sacred Places

An important dimension in my spiritual life is that of **space** – both my own inner space and that of my physical surroundings. It is true that my physical surroundings may be decided by someone else in some circumstances, a work-setting perhaps, but my inner reality is always mine: it can be anything I choose to make it. It need not be dictated by physical surroundings or role or status or wealth or health. Nothing external need be a controlling factor in **my** sacred space or with my connection to all that is.

There are, of course, many, many truly special places existing out in the world, and Rievaulx Abbey is a particularly powerful and significant one for me. Rievaulx is where I first experienced the wonderful sense of belonging to all that is, and that connection to everything around me and the universe as a whole. I usually spend one week twice a year at Rievaulx on self-directed retreats, which have always provided great insight, learning, and challenge. I find simply sitting in the Abbey, sometimes surrounded by others, sometimes with the entire site to myself, a nourishing and essential part of my life.

My relationship with the Abbey has changed over the years. Initially it was a place where I felt at home: a place of safety and acceptance; a place where I had to slow down and focus on deeper issues. This has never gone; it is more that other dimensions have appeared. I now know that I am part of the community at Rievaulx and that my presence is as positive an influence for the Abbey and those who work and visit there as the Abbey is for me. Further, there have been countless occasions where 'chance' conversations with visitors led to healing meetings. In this way I learned yet more about how my stillness and my presence is all that is needed for the Divine to use in whatever way is needed at that time by that person in those circumstances.

In addition to Rievaulx, other significant and powerful places have included the temple in Singapore, Castlerigg Stone Circle in Cumbria, **any** hilly/mountainous area, Lastingham Church Crypt; my garden. I find that places like this draw me to them.

Another example is Machu Picchu in Peru. I had been aware of the pull of Machu Picchu for a number of years and by 2006 I could deny it no longer. So in 2007, with two friends (and a guide), I walked the short Inca Trail and spent two days at Machu Picchu before exploring other parts of the country. The Trail became more of a trial – it was incredibly hot with the sun beating relentlessly down as we climbed a steep, steep path consisting of hundreds upon hundreds of high stone steps for over six hours before beginning to level off. I was dehydrated (having lost my bottle of water down the hill!); I was exhausted and seriously wondered if I would survive the trek. At my lowest point I was visited by Wolf – one of my Power Animals – and he carried me on his back for a considerable distance. The experience with Wolf was amazing: I began to breathe more freely; I re-discovered my walking rhythm; the nausea and dizziness left me; the craving for water diminished.

Later we came upon the most glorious sight of a fast flowing waterfall and, to add to my relief, we entered shady trees thus escaping the fiery sun for the first time since setting off hours earlier. It was at the waterfall that I encountered another angel, in the form of a Trail guide. Our own guide was a long way behind

with one of our threesome who was finding the trek incredibly hard (the two of us had decided we needed to maintain our own rhythm as best we could and, as a consequence, we were a considerable distance in front of them). The guide that caught up with us at the waterfall gave me some of her water; plenty to keep me going until we reached the refreshment place at the highest point of the Trail, where we were due to have a break and where I would be able to re-hydrate. She went out of her way to check we were OK and ensured we were on the right path.

In addition to all this, early the next morning we went up the mountain (by bus!) to watch the sun rise over Machu Picchu. Two of us spent the morning in meditation; a wholly remarkable experience and time together. The following afternoon as we left the sacred site for the last time, I was overcome by emotion. I did not want to leave; I did not want to return to the valley below. Then I had the clear, certain knowing that the beings I had encountered at Machu Picchu would be accompanying me on my journey – not just for now but for always – and also that my presence would remain with them at Machu Picchu. This was not a diminishing of either but an adding to; a level of consciousness that transcended time, physical form, geographical boundaries and realities. I felt so at home at Machu Picchu, and I am still aware of that presence, that level of connection. These experiences are now part of me and are integrated into my life and practice.

I believe that any space is sacred (hence including my garden in the list above); all things are sacred, all people are sacred, the whole universe is sacred and, since we are sacred, our bodies are, per se, sacred spaces so I take that sacredness wherever I go. Space does not need to be consecrated to be sacred; it does not need special ritual and it does not need separation from the rest of life. However, I believe all spaces can be enhanced by the intent of those in and around them, and I encountered one striking example of this during a visit to John Heron in Italy for the beginning of a long-term co-operative inquiry. I was struck by the way in which he had created a number of shrines around his grounds, each with a specific and different focus, that were incredibly powerful. Here was a living example of taking ordinary parts of a garden and enabling something extremely non-ordinary to develop.

Cape Reinga, at the very tip of New Zealand's North Island, is another profoundly significant sacred place. When I visited some years ago I knew little of the Cape's story but when I stepped off the bus it was like being 'zapped': I felt an overwhelming connection with life and death, the past, present and future. Our driver/tour guide briefly mentioned the Maori *Land of the Spirits*[18] and then went on to say that this is a topic he chooses not to talk about in any great detail. I was really struck by what he was saying so, in spite of his usual reticence, during lunch I found him by himself to ask if he would tell me more. I'm sure he recognised that my interest was far more than idle curiosity because we had a lengthy, really good conversation.

[18] The Cape is tremendously important to Maoris and their ritual surrounding death. For two days the dead person's spirit stays with the body; days 3-7 the spirit is finding its way through different realms to Spirit Bay (around Cape Reinga) and on day 9 the spirit is met by spirit guides who take it to the Point by the Sacred Tree.

The Power of Music

A very early and unexpected (to me) influence was music. In one counselling session Bryce suggested – actually he *told* me, in the nicest possible way – to listen to the second movement of Beethoven's violin concerto No. 2. At the time I thought it was strange that he had been so specific – the second movement. Well, I thought, this can't do any harm, so a few days later I listened to the music. It was one of the most haunting pieces of music I had ever heard.

I found it touched a part of me that I had been protecting so fiercely – my heart. I cried and cried. It was so moving and I still cannot explain how come – that language thing again. But I do know that the floodgates opened and that it was instrumental in leading me towards owning feelings and to having more of a feeling life than ever before.

I find that music takes me away from my everyday state and thus allows other things to enter in, whether they are feelings – tears, anger, joy, wonder, majesty, awe – or an awareness of other realities beyond my current understanding. My mood or state often determines the music I choose to listen to at any given moment: it might be to take me deeper into an already existing state, for meditation perhaps; it might be for healing; it might be to lift me out of a mood such as my tendency for melancholia; it might be to express the sense of joy that bubbles up or simply to dance to.

Films and Television

At first, I was very surprised when I discovered that, if I am sufficiently open to such events, anything can have an influence way beyond its apparent surface value – including television programmes, films, radio programmes and other ordinary aspects of day-to-day life. *Lord of the Rings,* Star Trek, SG-1, ER have all suddenly taken me to totally unexpected places through a phrase, a scene or even a word that has an impact way beyond its context.

A few months after I saw my transcended Self as part of the guided meditation on my own death, I was watching a science fiction programme called SG-1 where one of the characters, Daniel (the scientist working alongside the military), was transformed into his transcendent being. What struck me more than anything was that the way in which this was portrayed on the television was almost identical to my own images: the colours, the form, the sense of what the character was saying all mirrored my own experience. It was one of those 'spooky' moments.

A second example occurred during ER (an American hospital drama). The scenario was that of the hero doctor attempting to rescue someone from a burning building. As the building erupted in flames, I was transported to a place of fear and pain, and I became aware that I was a witch being burned at the stake. This was not the first occasion I'd had this experience but this time it took me so deeply into it physically, mentally and emotionally that I, in effect, relived the burning. It was a salutary experience but I learned a tremendous amount from it, not least that there is so much I do not understand and that there is so much the Church is not willing to either explore or acknowledge.

Even the theme music for a programme can be a stimulus; *Search for the Hero inside Yourself* (the theme music for one of the Star Trek spin off programmes), for example. It gave rise within me to a clear sense that the journey is about searching for my own hero within – I just need to find it and nurture it.

Drawing and Colour Work

I've always known that I could not draw or paint or use colour. I was told so in school and I was, not very tactfully, told that I would be better taking geography and history at GCE rather than art. A year later I was identified as colour blind[19] so how on earth could I ever have been expected to be good at art or painting? So, when Bryce (still my counsellor at this stage) suggested – strongly – that I *should* use paint and colour, I was particularly resistant. What was the point? I can't see colours and I knew I couldn't draw – I'd been told that often enough.

Yet this was not about producing pictures as such, rather it was about using colour, whether paint, crayons or pastels, in whatever way just came through. Like the writing, there was to be no planning of what to draw: no drafts; no colours chosen before beginning. This was another exercise in allowing my inner consciousness – my inner wisdom – to come through and be expressed out in the world.

In the event I agreed. The resulting pictures were striking and stark – all black and red – and seeing them was deeply affecting. I had not realised how angry I was still, or how dark, how black, my world was at that time.

I have kept many of my creations and when I was searching for something else completely different I came across them tucked away behind a chest of drawers. I was immediately distracted from my original search and spent the next hour or so looking through them all. I am very grateful that I began dating them fairly soon after that first challenge because I was able to see the timeline and the very clear transitions and changes in both style and colours used.

---

[19] My colour blindness (or, more accurately, colour deficiency) takes the form of being unable to distinguish colours that are similar in shade or depth.

Blacks and reds with straight lines like bars of a prison gave way to more gentle colours, sweeping shapes and a sense of freedom. The two drawings below are examples of the contrast and are indicative of what truly felt like a move out of my own self-imposed prison into freedom.

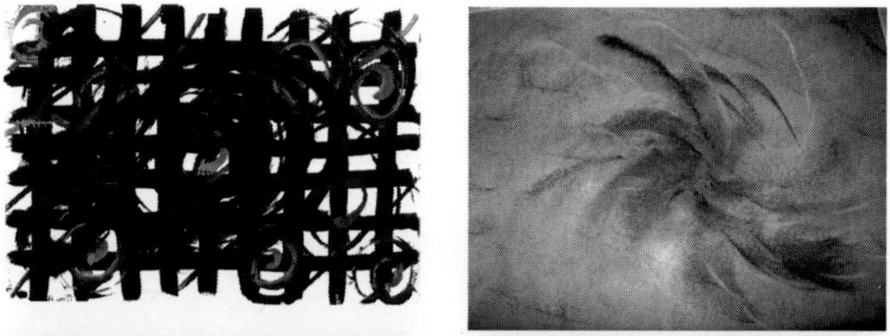

1993 2005

Figure 3: From Prison to Freedom

I found expressing the violent strong emotions through painting a very liberating experience. Now, I enjoy using pastels, allowing whatever colours and shapes to appear as they will, and I know I can see more colours now too.

Ritual and Shamanic Journeying

Since the springboard for my spiritual awakening was the Anglican Church, I am very familiar with formally organised and regimented ritual and ceremony. In considerable contrast to this background, the rituals I use in my own practice are self-initiated and self-created.

I allow rituals to unfold organically out of specific circumstances, events or needs. They may be to mark significant transitions and important events, or to celebrate times of breakthrough in my learning, understanding and insights. They may be to acknowledge certain times of the year, such as significant dates, the winter and summer solstices, the spring equinox. In addition, ritual has been invaluable to me as part of letting go processes, notably in the days of working through the grief around Neil, relinquishing outdated patterns, and, in more recent times, the death of my mother in November 2009.

In addition to these stimuli, I sometimes receive the impulse to undertake a ritual through dreams, or a word someone says, or something I read, or an image or vision. Whatever the 'something' is that sparks the notion of a ritual, I've learned to follow it even though I may not know why or what the main focus might be. I've discovered that the ritual itself will reveal more of how come it was important to do it. Further, I delight in the discovery that being part of a group where a ritual evolves organically is an incredibly powerful experience.

I have undertaken numerous shamanic style journeys as a result of stimuli similar to those for rituals. The knowledge I gain from these experiences is always invaluable, even when the journey may have been challenging. In some of my first journeys into other realms, I was scared of how far I was travelling and wondered if I would ever find my way back, but once I've entered that state all fear goes and all is as it is meant to be. If I didn't come back, then that is OK too. That sense of "...all shall be well, and all shall be well, and all manner of things shall be well" (Julian of Norwich) has grown in me over the years and the fear of journeying diminished.

I have always found it both helpful and important to have a witness during these journeys, and it has been hugely beneficial to have someone with whom I can talk through insights and experiences, especially when the conversation takes place whilst still in the heightened state.

Silence and Stillness

Silence is a potent medium and it can 'speak volumes'. The philosopher, George Steiner, observed that language can only deal with a small, restricted part of reality and that "presumably the larger part is silence".

> "We need silence to be able to touch souls." **Mother Teresa**

There are fewer and fewer places in our culture where there is quiet, let alone silence; it is almost as though the silence has to be filled for fear of what might happen. Silence is an amazing opportunity for insights and understandings to surface, equally, however, it is also a place where difficult emotions or thoughts can surface.

Go to a Tree

Go to a tree in silence
You will find
In the soft eloquence
Of bud and leaf
Serenity beyond the voice
Of grief
And faith beyond the reach
Of humankind.
Man spends his noisy days
In search of gain
While trees find God
In sunlight
Soil and rain

Unknown

For me stillness and silence have often travelled hand in hand – though they do not have to. I can find stillness in activity too, but it took me quite some time to distinguish between running away – from myself – into activity, and activity being a vehicle to reach that place of stillness within. Walking, gardening, and listening to music are just three ways in which I can be in that place of inner stillness and be receptive to the universe whilst also being involved in an activity. I can also experience a wonderful sense of stillness amidst noise and activity going on around me.

However I find it, I know that a joyous impact of my journey is my increased capacity to be still; to simply be with who I am and how I am at a given moment. To be still and allow what will be to emerge and to unfold has become a major feature of my life. Sitting with expectancy, with intent or just being in my surroundings is essential, wherever I find myself. It is in this stillness that I can reach my innermost being and learn yet more about who I truly am.

Archetypes, Temperaments and Myths

Ancient traditions and wisdoms have always been passed down through the generations, usually by word of mouth or by passing knowledge from one chosen person to the next, but, sadly, many are becoming lost or sidelined. Yet, even though they are mainly discounted in our modern cultures, they remain intensely creative and powerful ways of understanding our world and ourselves, whether they are recognised in mainstream traditions or not.

Archetypes are just one of these ancient traditions and wisdom. They encompass universal relationships, roles, traits and are part of that collective consciousness to which we are all connected. Each of us will experience these archetypes and make our connection with the collective unconscious in our own way and from our own perspective. Carol Pearson describes this as follows:

> "1. Spiritual seekers may conceive of archetypes as gods and goddesses, encoded in the collective unconscious, whom we scorn at our risk.
>
> 2. Academics or other rationalists... may conceive of archetypes as controlling paradigms or metaphors, the invisible patterns in the mind that control how we experience the world.

3. Scientists may see archetypes as being similar to holograms and the process of identifying them as similar to other scientific processes.
4. People who are committed to religious positions that emphasize one God... the archetypes are like different facets of that God, accessible to the psyche's capacity to imagine numinous reality.
5. Finally, people who are interested in human growth and development may understand the archetypes as guides on our journeys. The archetypes together teach us how to live. ...all the archetypes live within us. That means we all have this full human potential within ourselves."

Carol Pearson, *Awakening the Heroes Within,* p281. HarperSanFrancisco, 1991.

I have found archetypal imagery to be a very useful resource, and being aware of archetypal forces and influences enables me to gain greater understanding of my role, my patterns, my strengths as well as those areas I may wish to develop further.

The Temperaments[20] (sometimes called the four humours) are Greek in origin and they formed an early method for thinking about and characterising people, continuing in popular use even as late as the time of Shakespeare. I have found that exploring the four Temperaments (Choleric, Sanguine, Phlegmatic and Melancholic) has greatly increased my understanding about how come I operate in the way I do. Studying how the four relate to one another, the points of contact and the areas in which they do not sit well together, also gave me considerable insight into how I relate to other people, whether of the same or a different temperament.

[20] Temperament: ...in psychology, an aspect of personality concerned with emotional dispositions and reactions and their speed and intensity; the term often is used to refer to the prevailing mood or mood pattern of a person (Encyclopaedia Britannica).

> "The melancholic does not feel at home among a crowd for any length of time; they love silence and solitude."
>
> **Bryce Taylor and Nick Ellerby,** *Discovering the Temperaments,* p37. Oasis Press, 2004.

This is a pretty good description of my preference! Melancholic was very clearly my dominant temperament, which goes a long way to explaining my attention to detail, my perception and intuition, my organisational skills and my capacity to plan, and my pre-disposition to stillness and contemplation. It also explained my need to find just the *right* word, my occasional lapse into melancholy, my self-critical tendency and discounting of achievements in a way that I do not apply to others.

It has been valuable to explore and identify those parts of the Melancholic that are not helpful or which can get in the way of my relationships so that I can then modify or let them go. Further, recognising the qualities that I wished to cultivate in my two less dominant temperaments (choleric and sanguine) enables me to become more balanced and have more options in responding to people and situations.

Divination Tools

I use a variety of tools for guidance, teaching or when looking for insight and clarity, including Medicine Cards, Runes, Archetype cards, Mythic Tarot, Osho Tarot, the Mayan Oracle, dowsing with a crystal, Angel cards. There are many, many tools of this nature from different parts of the world based upon ancient wisdoms within wide-ranging cultures, belief systems and philosophies. Each in their own way gives insight into the question I hold in mind or the issue that is most present. Each is different in approach and style yet each has been incredibly useful to me.

When I first began using divination cards, I noticed that I had a tendency to favour some over others: eagle being more desirable than skunk, say – not a particularly enlightened way of seeking wisdom! It is true, however, that whatever card I've taken, especially when 'reversed' (upside down), it has always been useful. Sometimes I have gained insight into where I am holding back; other times I have received affirmation of where I am and shifts made; on other occasions I am challenged to look at a familiar concept or way of operating from a new perspective.

Sometimes I take a single card with a question in mind; sometimes I do spreads looking at issues more fully; then there are those times when I have done a pathway spread (the different styles have their own names for a selection of cards that addresses the person's whole life, which is usually only done once). Having drawn my card(s) the process I follow is threefold:

1. I sit with the cards for a while just allowing myself to be still with them.
2. I read whatever commentary is available (often making notes).
3. I meditate/contemplate on the cards and the commentary.

When I am considering a question or a situation, I find that I am drawn to a particular tool; it is not a conscious decision and I have learned to trust that instinct and intuition more fully. Whichever system 'calls' me, for greatest effectiveness I need to approach it with an open mind without having a specific answer or a preferred outcome already worked out. This enables an emergent process to take place where my own inner wisdom can come through to illuminate the learning and the understanding to be gained.

Reading

Reading is important and many books have 'spoken' to me over the years. Early in my awakening *The Hidden Journey* (Andrew Harvey) was especially influential in shifting my attitude towards what was happening in my life. In the book, he describes a number of his transpersonal experiences and as I was reading it I was saying to myself things like: 'Yes, I've seen that'; 'Yes, I've experienced that, too'. It gave me a tremendous boost to know that here was someone else who was having similar experiences and, crucially, who was not afraid of this being known by countless other people.

Some books gave me information about different approaches, different traditions, different views; some inspired; some challenged; some affirmed where I was; some were able to express what I had been unable to find words for; some made me laugh and were able to lighten my mood. Some even managed to hold all of this. The books varied in category, too, from poetry to inspirational writing, to academic and information-giving, to life-stories, to fiction.

Finding *my* Practice

All of these influences and experiences have been part of my journey and thus have been part of an on-going process of finding my practice. I had many questions: What will be *my* preferred style of choice? How will I fulfil my destiny? How will I honour who I know myself to be? Do I want/need to be part of a particular tradition? Will I undertake some form of training in a given approach? How will I know if I am developing in my spiritual understanding? How will I know the 'right' path for me? Do I need a teacher/mentor/group? How will I find one (or more)?

I valued all these questions – and more – for what they taught me about my way forward as they helped me form the basis of a developing practice. On the other hand, I was aware it was important not to let such questions get so much of a hold and so much control that I was lost in *thinking about* what to do and never actually doing anything.

Exploring many forms of practice to connect with myself and others was a good starting point, but I needed to be aware that flitting from one to another could be yet another form of sabotage if it meant that I did not take hold of something firmly and with commitment. I found that I needed both discipline and commitment in order to hold to my own practice. In time, I needed fewer and fewer specific conditions, less conscious preparation, and I entered into altered states more easily and more immediately in my everyday life.

I am also very familiar with the sabotage of 'not knowing how to'. It is as though I was desperate for a step-by-step guide: this is how to do this; if I do this, then 'that' will happen and then I do this, then that and behold I will be enlightened! I parody the process to make a point, but it is true that the 'manual' is a very attractive idea in the delusion that it will make my journey easier, simpler, and more straightforward. I soon discovered that not knowing how to do something is no excuse.

In this work I learn by experience; by taking those leaps into the unknown; by having a go at what seems and feels to be the right thing for me to grasp hold of at that moment. Once I gained that sense of awareness of a journey ahead and once I made a commitment to myself in that, then I needed to just take it on, grasp the nettle as it were, and get on with it.

It is very easy to become seduced by a particular form of practice, whether that be a certain style of meditation, a particular belief system, a ritual of some kind or any of the myriad approaches available today. Although I knew it was crucial to develop a form of practice, I also knew it was equally crucial – if not more so – to remember that the practice is not the focus of the work. The practice or the place or the discipline or the ritual is not the outcome; the practice is only the vehicle by which I enter and continue the work. What is important is the outlet and opportunity my practices give me to learn more, to contribute more to the universe, to become who I was born to be.

Finding and developing my own path through the 'forest' has been and still is a major piece of work. There are many variations on themes 'out there' and it is important for me to be aware and ensure that anyone I choose to work with fits for me. There are still people who seek followers or disciples as part of their own ego trip – and it is not always easy to see this in the first instance. As I travel along and as I grow to trust my own inner wisdom, I am able to discern those paths and approaches that work for me, as well as the people that are genuine; people that are on their own journey and who might travel with me for a while in whatever capacity is appropriate for us both in this moment.

Trial and error, openness and flexibility all assisted me to find the most beneficial, challenging and appropriate practice for me. Some aspects change as I change, some are less frequently used whilst some have remained constant and are the bedrock of my practice – notably meditation, sitting with intent, spirit guides and allies, shamanic journeying, rituals, use of myth and archetypes, and a variety of cards. Freedom to go with what my inner being is telling me is critical. Freedom in choice of how I respond to what I increasingly know is equally critical. All of these come through having my journey as *the* priority in my life and through the discipline of my practice.

8

Healing through Meeting

Introduction

Of all the significant influences and experiences I celebrate in my journey, the single most outstanding and important dimension is that of the people who have travelled alongside me in some way and this is why the final chapter is dedicated to them. Their contributions have been critical from the very beginning, remaining so to this day. Some have met me in my pain and enabled me to find a way through; some have introduced me to new routes of practice; some have given me friendship and support; some have challenged and encouraged; some have played different roles in different situations and at different times. It is essential to me that I honour the part they have played and acknowledge their impact upon me.

The relationships have ranged from formal helping situations to friends (and even those I had viewed as possible enemies); from neighbours to priests; from Allies[21] (in the Carlos Castaneda sense of the word) to spontaneous, momentary meetings with total

[21] "The ally is the means by which the warrior transcends the realm of ordinary reality... a power capable of transporting a man beyond the boundaries of himself." Carlos Casteneda.

strangers; from an astrologer to a doctor of Chinese medicine; from animal spirit guides to my guardian angel and beings in other realms; from counsellor to teacher, guide, mentor and fellow traveller.

It is only in retrospect I can recognise that *healing through meeting*[22] is a vital element running through the significant and influential relationships on my journey. It has been the times I have been met and been heard in the fullest way possible by an other that has enabled me to step into more of who I am: to be honest about who I am; to accept challenge; to begin to recognise my gifts and my skills; to learn to trust; to take steps that might seem risky or fearful; to own and acknowledge those areas of my life that are in need of more light, more attention. All of this without feeling put down, inferior, a failure, or that any perceived difficulty is a sign that the rest of my journey is invalid.

Through these kinds of meetings, I learned a great deal about inhabiting a stance of not having to be perfect but, rather, being able simply to be true to myself, especially by having this attitude role-modelled to me. At times, it has been very difficult to maintain this with the noise of my inner critic, which can still sometimes interfere with comparisons, put downs, and the language of 'not-good-enough-land'.

I recognise that I have been incredibly fortunate in meeting a number of people who are free enough in themselves to allow me to be free also and, more, to encourage my freedom; secure enough in their own journeys to enable me to step into mine – however

---

[22] 'Healing through meeting' is a phrase I first heard from Bryce Taylor. For me, it encapsulates the sense that it is the willingness of the person offering support or help to truly meet, be present to and fully with the other in relationship that is so important.

different that might be from their own path or from what steps they thought I needed or was ready to take.

Travelling with An Other

An important learning for me was that as I travelled further along my path, there were fewer people to share it with, therefore it became increasingly important to me to have a place where I could talk about my experiences, my learning, my knowing – both of the light and the dark.

I have found it to be an absolute joy to have someone who can share, to a degree, the experiences of entering and experiencing altered states with all the attendant difficulties, wonder, bliss and anxieties. It is affirming to have someone who is able to normalise such experiences and give them context or a different perspective, if needed. I certainly did – and do.

In addition, it is an opportunity for loving challenge if what I describe does not seem congruent to the person listening. Congruence between what I *say* I experience, what I *do* in those other realms, how I *operate* on a day-to-day basis and how others experience me is important. Congruence is not about being perfect and getting things 'right' but is about being genuine and living what I espouse; it is about being real and straight in my relationships with others and myself. This is a major part of the reality check. I am not saying that for my experiences to be authentic I must be liked by everyone in some kind of utopian frenzy of 'niceness', it is more that there is that sense of 'walk matching talk' and a travel companion can note inconsistencies, challenge incongruences.

Further, they can highlight, acknowledge and celebrate shifts, transitions and transformations. I have always found it easier to own my 'failings' and shortcomings far more readily and quickly than to recognise and claim the positive shifts and steps that I have taken.

Each of us, I believe, will find our own relationship with those we meet along the way: some we might help; some will help us; with yet others we might enter into a more formal student/teacher relationship. There are teachers who are truly inspirational, though they may or may not be formally described as teachers. They are people, however, to whom I feel drawn and from whom I wish to learn. They may have ideas I find intriguing; they may promote a way of life that I wish to experience and explore; they may have a role within a particular ritual or approach into which I wish to enter more deeply.

Transmitting information, enabling others to learn, assisting others to take on their potential, travelling alongside others are all important and valued roles. However, with such recognition and influence comes responsibility to ensure they give their students space to learn what they (the students) need to learn and to travel in the direction they need to travel rather than some form of blind obedience because the 'teacher knows best'.

Finding my Teacher/Guides

Searching for a teacher takes many forms. Animal cards, tarot, cards of many kinds, meditation, journeying, guided visualisation, reading, Runes, dowsing, dreams, are but a few examples. Regardless of the tool being used, it is crucial for me simply to hold an intent: an intent of meeting and finding the teacher I need and then trusting the process and the universe. Being uninvested in who might come my way is an important aspect of this strategy since I have come to realise that my teachers often take very unexpected forms: the person I would least expect; the direction or approach I had never considered previously. Listening to my own inner wisdom in this way is a powerful tool.

In many ways there cannot be a CV or a list of qualifications for a teacher or guide; everyone's needs are so unique that it would be both undesirable and impossible to have a list of criteria. However, certain qualities, certain characteristics, are important to me. It is of paramount importance, for example, that I feel safe enough to do whatever I need to do in order to benefit from the relationship. It is crucial that I feel 'held' by the person but not that they will collude in keeping me where I am because they, perhaps, are not at ease with strong emotions, or they cannot hear very different experiences from their own, or they need me to be a certain way. I also need them to be able to let go of their own agenda, have no attachment to where I might go, and know that they do not have to 'get it right' or 'make it better'.

Many of my significant, overtly helping relationships began through recommendations from others, yet whether the relationship developed was primarily dependent upon my own response to the person. An unmoveable principle for me must be my own instincts and intuition since it is the relationship between us that is the key to whether a connection will be useful, effective and positive. I have to trust myself enough that I will know whether a person, a tradition, a style, a guide of any kind is right for me. Only I can determine whether the other – whoever or whatever it is – is going to be a positive influence for me and is going to enable me to find the path that is mine in the way that is mine. Taking this responsibility for my choice of teacher is essential so that I maintain my integrity within any relationships I enter.

The remainder of this chapter gives a flavour of the way in which I met the key people, teachers and guides who have travelled (some of whom still travel) alongside me in my explorations, my quest, and my searchings. It is largely in chronological order, except for the one person who has been with me from almost the very beginning. This relationship and his presence have been a constant inspiration and grounding force for me, so in order to honour his role, I have chosen to end the chapter with it.

The Church

One form of helping was the connections I had through the Church. Although we were in an interregnum (i.e. we had no priest) when Neil died, three other priests within the area took me 'under their wings' in quite delightful ways. In addition, the priest who had moved on a few months previously invited me on a regular basis to his new parishes in North Yorkshire. It was very therapeutic to be walking in the hills with him and his dogs – which I'd taken out for walks whilst they were still in my parish. Those conversations were an open opportunity for me to rail against God, question what had happened, the place of faith and all those questions that naturally arise in times of grief and stress.

When the new priest arrived it was clear very early on that we could work well together and have a good personal and professional relationship. The conversations that followed – and there were many – were truly healing. I often dropped in at the Vicarage on my way back from a counselling session to talk through what I'd experienced, what I'd heard, what I was thinking. I was very fortunate, too, that he was open to my challenges concerning the dogma and the traditions of the church. As I began the long journey into trusting my own experiences and my own intuition, he was open to hearing my version of what being a Christian meant – or no longer meant – to me.

The Church certainly was an invaluable source of personal support especially in the early days after Neil's death, yet it also, paradoxically, became something of a straitjacket. Nonetheless, I do know that both parishes enfolded me in a way that was nourishing and compassionate, and I will always be very thankful for this.

Community Psychiatric Nurse

My initial need for formal helping came out of a place of deep despair and grief and I now know it also enabled me to begin to see the possibilities for a different way of being. I was referred to a CPN (Paul) by my GP some three months after Neil died. Paul's approach was alien to me in so many ways. He actually wanted me to express my anger; he encouraged me to tell him *exactly* how I was feeling – he was not content with 'I'm doing OK' or 'I'm fine'.

I very soon came to see him as a parrot on my shoulder; *my* Parrot. I could hear him constantly giving me the 'antidote' to my patterns, my messages; encouraging me to be more open; telling me to allow people to see more of me and to know more of me. In a less than guarded moment I even told him this and, although I expected a rebuff of some kind, he simply laughed and said he thought it was a great image.

He set me a number of homework tasks such as gathering together all the funeral notices and all the letters and cards I had received to take with me to read to him during the next session. Another task included writing a letter to Neil saying 'goodbye'; a letter no one else would ever see so I could be completely open and free – none of my usual editing before speaking. However, it didn't work out that way since he insisted I read it out loud – all of it. It was one of those occasions when I felt Paul was extremely devious, but for which I am now grateful.

Further tasks included writing 'My Secrets' and 'What I would lose if I spoke about them'; 'What I want from a relationship' and 'What I will allow myself'; 'Hellos' and 'Goodbyes'. In all these the emphasis was always on honesty with myself, acceptance of how I was feeling, non-avoidance of difficulties and issues, as well as challenges to look after myself more with regard to eating and sleeping. But perhaps the biggest challenge he set me – and for which he presented an excellent role model – was to trust: to trust him; to trust myself.

In addition to all this he began the opening to a sexual life and world I had never considered. One memorable event was a book[23] he put through my letter box with a note saying:

"P160, The Zoo and anything else in the book you wish to read you may find amusing.

1. If you feel shocked, ask yourself what about and where the messages come from.
2. If excited, acknowledge it, store it for possible future exploration, after all these are female fantasies (men have similar ones).

Have a good Christmas. The Parrot

PS Optional reading not a homework!"

There were other books, too, and it was sometimes excruciatingly, embarrassingly amazing to hear him talk freely about sexuality, sex and all that this meant with regard to my losing a partner and my own 'hang-ups', repression and so on. So Paul began an opening and flowering which took many years to come to fruition.

[23] The book was *My Secret Garden*, Nancy Friday, Quartet Books Ltd, 1976.

Although there felt to be no overt, explicit spiritual dimension to this relationship, it holds a powerful place in my journey simply because, without meeting Paul, without his encouragement – bullying, I sometimes thought of it at the time – and without his commitment and willingness to stay with this closed-down, reluctant and resistant client, I could not have taken the following steps. He began the process of breaching the dam; enabling me to feel rather than always to be in my head. Further, it was at his suggestion that I began a six month counselling skills course – an event which led to meeting with the man who was to become my counsellor, my teacher, my mentor, my fellow traveller.

Informal Helping

Whilst more formal helping relationships were taking place there were other, less formal places where I gained great support and assistance. I use the term 'informal' caring or helping to describe the support given by friends, family, colleagues and neighbours in often ad hoc ways. I felt this very strongly in the village – the strength of a smaller community – when Neil died. I had places where I could just drop in for a cup of tea or coffee; there were friends who would ring to see how I was, others who dropped by, others who invited me for meals and one who brought prepared meals to me; there were yet others I simply continued to play hockey with. All were life-savers in their own way.

There are two families in particular who took me into their midst. I was invited into their homes and was accepted as a member of their extended families – a truly nurturing and supporting experience. These were places where I learned more about not needing to hide behind masks. If I was so fatigued I needed to sleep, I did so; if I was sad it was OK to let that be known and seen. One of these families has moved on, children no longer 'children' but grown adults with homes and partners of their own, but the memories are still there. The other family still feels like a second home and it is a real privilege to be part of both their family celebrations and their more difficult times.

In addition to this, I am now in the fortunate place of having a small number of people with whom I can share so much more of my journey than ever before. The annual Retreat I have attended for over a decade, for example, has given me opportunities to speak as much or as little as I choose, to speak with others, to listen to others. It is a unique and invaluable space that I cherish and the relationships I have developed on the Retreats are on-going, mutual and co-creative.

As part of an important realisation that I need to be more open and less reticent concerning how much I put out about my journey, I have a 'contract' with a few people to talk in more depth of my experiences and the learning I glean from them.

Massage Practitioner

Soon after the end of the counselling skills course that Paul recommended, I began to see a massage practitioner (Maggie) at the suggestion of Bryce. She had a truly significant impact on me through enabling me to become aware of my body, all it holds and, through this awareness, to begin to release some of my tensions and fears.

Equally significant for me is that I experienced her as a woman who was not afraid of her own body – or mine; a woman who was not afraid of her power; a woman who was not afraid of her influence with people and, perhaps even more than any of those, she saw in me things I was completely blind to.

Further, here was someone who did not hide behind roles or status, or hold herself distant from the 'client', rather she was fully present (though I could not have expressed it in this way at that time) with me, fully accepting of me and so the space was created for me to feel free too. And it was at her suggestion that I put my hands on her, an event that opened a whole new dimension for me i.e. my capacity for healing and working with energy.

Another result of this connection was that I attended a nine month therapeutic massage training course which qualified me to work as a self-employed massage practitioner alongside my counselling work. During and after this training, it was a joy and a privilege to be asked to give her bodywork sessions, which continued until she emigrated from the UK to New Zealand. I learned a tremendous amount from her, for which I will always be grateful.

Psychotherapist and Bodywork Practitioner

This helping relationship was with the facilitator of my massage training course (Sean). During the nine month course, I learned much about anatomy, the various styles of massage and the practicalities of working in this way with other people. However, learning yet more about how my body holds memories, how much tension my body can hold and how unaware of that I can be, was of even greater value. Finally, I was also beginning to accept that I have considerable capacity for knowing where to put my hands for healing as well as intuitively being able to work at the appropriate depth for each person.

Towards the end of this training course (late 1993), I was making huge changes in my world: I left full-time teaching and I embarked upon a two year course entitled The Practice of Counselling and the Management of Change (PCMC). In addition to being a completely new venture, this course was also the catalyst for a shift in my relationship with Bryce. The conditions of PCMC stated that a participant could not be in a counselling relationship with one of the course facilitators so this ended the formal helping relationship, because Bryce would be a visiting facilitator for one of the weekends.

A further PCMC condition stated that participants had to be in a counselling relationship during the first year, at least, of the course. I felt at ease with Sean and felt I had a good connection with him during the massage training course so, because he was a psychotherapist in addition to his massage training qualifications, I began working with him. My sessions with him combined deeper bodywork, addressing patterns, space to work though issues and concerns that arose during PCMC along with opportunities to explore more of what it means to me to be a woman. A truly eye-opening and valuable time.

Spirit Guides and Helpers

Finding my spirit guides, my animal guides, my allies, helpers and my guardian angel has been a very different experience to that of finding human teachers. It was some time into my journey before I became aware of the possibilities for such entities to be part of my life, for the potential for them to teach, to support, to guide me in ways that are perhaps not as tangible as those for a living human being but which, nevertheless, are very significant parts of my consciousness.

My first clear awareness of having some entity with me was the presence of my guardian angel, and the transition to taking on the role of guardian angel for others was a real milestone for me. It was a clear indication of how my experiences and learning then become available for the service of others.

I have also felt the presence of malevolent, dangerous entities. The first time I experienced this was when I was out for a walk in the countryside near where I live. I felt their presence shadowing me; moving parallel to me but a bit apart. This was the catalyst for beginning to explore the notion of being open to possibilities yet not necessarily allowing everything in regardless of nature or intention, thus contributing towards my developing greater discernment.

I met my three Animal guides at different times and in different ways: one through an early piece of creative writing; one through a shamanic journey; one through a meeting in nature. None of these three events was entered into with a view to finding an animal guide yet that is what occurred and they are still with me. Each has very different qualities and each has, therefore, taught me different things and drawn my attention to different aspects of my life, my potential, the areas I need to address and the gifts I have that I might not be valuing sufficiently.

Other spirit beings I have met through journeys have had varying roles; some teaching me how to journey; some giving me support in those journeys; some welcoming me into this dimension; some with me to celebrate the transformation of my being; some are my fellow spirit callers and workers.

Astrologer

At about the time I was ending the massage training course, leaving teaching, beginning PCMC and changing counsellors, Bryce suggested I go to see an astrologer, Lyn Birkbeck. I was somewhat sceptical but I was also intrigued and curious as to what it might reveal or highlight. The appointment was made and the only information Lyn requested in order to prepare my chart was the date, time and place of my birth.

So, a few weeks later I drove to Keswick to see him. This was no hardship since I have felt at home amongst the mountains of the Lake District for many years, and now realise that mountains anywhere in the world hold a particular draw and connection for me. I arrived feeling nervous; uncertain what to expect. In the event, it exceeded anything I could possibly have anticipated. From the very first moment I experienced him as a warm, insightful and accepting person. As the session progressed I was very struck by what he was saying. The phrase, 'How on earth could he know that?' was a regular feature of my thoughts and my reflections.

He 'knew' that it was likely I would be involved with teaching, with preaching, that the spiritual dimension of my life would be of paramount importance, and that physical difficulties would be strongly held in my body. I was pretty staggered by this since, of course, it was all absolutely true. I was just at the beginning of the slide into fatigue – though I was unaware of it at that time; I was a Reader; I had been a full time teacher for well over twenty years. The conversation was even more important to me in many ways than the chart itself because it illuminated and expanded that information. Since he records conversations, I was able to listen to it again on my way home – a really useful way of re-entering the space and reflecting more deeply on what he said. I have reproduced a fraction of it here as an indication of the depth of the observations.

> "It is useful because it is saying your intuition is firing quite well and so you should be storing up what it is telling you because you are going to need it! The clarity you are gaining is not just for the ride, it is very important. You are stocking up provisions for the journey in a way."

"This is about meeting fate half-way rather than letting it beat you to the punch entirely. It is a co-creation."

"The thing is, though, once you have taken that step of awareness, I suppose you might call it, it changes the ball game. And you can't go back. It is not possible to put the genie back in the bottle. The path one has set oneself on prevails and astrology tells you the twists and turns; basically Pluto and Jupiter are so important to you because Jupiter is the planet of beliefs and God, the one who espouses what they believe in. You're a brilliant potential sorcerer."

"It is back to the relationship between you and the universe, you and God. Pluto empowers or destroys or both. It does not like you to tread some kind of middle ground. It is a very extreme planet. It is the creator and the destroyer so it is saying you are either going to empower and transform and intensify that religious aspect to yourself, or parts of it are going to be knocked off."

Conversations with Lyn over the years since that first visit have all been very relevant and have highlighted important issues: use and abuse of power; my potential; that my destiny is to be a shaman; that I am a guardian of the power and the knowledge; that I need to work out what I am willing to stand up and out for (my shield); that I am destined to be 'out on the edge'; that one of my prime roles is bringing the unseen realm into the seen.

In one meeting, he gave me a phrase that spoke to my potential – *receive in order to transmit*; another challenge to begin to take on who I truly am and to be willing to explore those possibilities. The idea of receiving and then transmitting has other meanings for me too. As I have travelled along and been accompanied by loving, challenging teachers and allies, so now I find that I am entering into that role for others.

I have felt challenged by what he uncovers and what he brings to the light, in a clear yet uninvested way; challenged to take on the roles my chart indicated; challenged to own more of who I have the potential to be; challenged to step into the unknown; challenged to recognise my place in the universe. Aspects of my 'make-up', such as my fear that I would abuse the power I have (because I have in previous lives), and my need for external approval were evident in various planetary alignments. As well as enabling me to understand these features, everything I heard and learned gave me a gateway to moving beyond such restrictions. I have always felt affirmed and supported by him in my journey.

As the years progressed, the conversations increasingly focussed upon spiritual realms, other beings, how we are all part of the same, and how I was finding my place in all that. I found these conversations liberating and such a good place to 'practise' being less fearful of talking about the experiences I was having. Here was another place – albeit only once a year – where it was OK to be open and it was more than OK to be exactly how I was feeling at that particular moment. Another place of healing though meeting.

Doctor of Chinese Medicine

This particular 'healing meeting' began in 2001 as a need for relief from a constant and painful sinus problem. My GP had informed me that surgery was the only viable next step, but I wanted to avoid surgical and medical intervention unless absolutely necessary. A friend recommended acupuncture since she had had a similar problem and it had helped her. Like Lyn, this was another new venture and with trepidation I went to see Phil, a doctor of Chinese Medicine.

The acupuncture had an immediate impact upon the sinuses and related symptoms for which I was – and still am – immensely grateful. It has also helped with my chronic lack of sleep, with emergency pain relief when I ruptured ligaments in my back, and with my overall health and well-being. It is difficult, if not impossible, to isolate one particular cause for the shift in my physical well-being following my period of debilitating fatigue but I do know that Phil has played a major role in that. Here is somewhere else where my feelings are acceptable (and accepted); where it is desirable to be how I am feeling at any given moment rather than wearing the masks of pretence.

Even though the sessions have never been just about the physical, over the years the balance has shifted much more towards the spiritual, personal journey kinds of conversations, whilst still addressing any physical issues. It took me a while to realise just what a safe place this was to talk about my experiences; that here was someone else who is accepting, non-judgemental. Here is a space where I am free to describe my journeys, the other realm 'work', the meetings with beings, guides, teachers.

There were occasions when we discovered that words got in the way. Because we were coming from different backgrounds we used different words, different reference systems, and common understanding occasionally seemed hard to come by. However, one thing I learned is that my drive, my need, to find exactly the right word can exclude other possibilities. I began to hear more of the meaning, the quality of what we were talking about rather than needing to be absolutely specific and finding the right phrase or the absolutely right word.

Phil is very insightful and, because he is not invested in my journey or my choices, he has no agenda and is free in how he offers suggestions – and challenges! There have been challenges for me to be less reticent when talking about my journey – this is an on-going process for me; there have been challenges to be less cautious in what I take on in my 'travels'; there have been challenges to accept my qualities, my gifts, my knowledge and my awareness.

He is a registered NES (Nutri-Energetics Systems) practitioner and part of this way of working entails identifying areas that need to be addressed and then recommending appropriate remedies (called Infoceuticals). Phil then often dowses[24] to confirm whether I need them or not and I have discovered that I know intuitively which remedies I need and which I don't simply by having them by my hand. At first I did not trust my own assessments and even now it is really useful to have the confirmation of Phil's dowsing. In this way I have learned to trust myself more: to trust myself to know what is right for me; to trust my intuition; to trust my instincts; to trust that I know what I need, don't need.

We have discovered that in some ways we are energetically linked: we are aware of each other in other realms; we have the capacity to work with each other in those realms. There is connection when we are not in each other's presence and there is a link in dream worlds. Phil asks me to undertake journeys for him, especially when I am away at Rievaulx but at other times too. When he first suggested this I was tentative in the way I fedback the insights and information I had received for him, particularly if I felt it might be challenging or appear directive. The observation

[24] To dowse is to search, with the aid of simple hand held tools or instruments (Phil uses a crystal) for that which is otherwise hidden from view or knowledge. Major-General Jim Scott-Eliot, in his book *Dowsing - One Man's Way*, describes it as: "The ability to use a Natural Sensitivity which enables us to know things we cannot know by the use of the day to day brain or by learning, by experience, or by the use of the five physical senses."

I received from him in return was that everything I come back with is always relevant, is always spot on and is always useful. Hearing this kind of affirmative and straight response was a further opportunity for me to re-assess my own beliefs about my capacity for that kind of work.

As I become more aware, more open and more centred, less fearful of the world, I feel that my own inner wisdom is so much more accessible. Learning to trust my inner wisdom and being able to respond from this place, rather than fear-driven or pattern-driven places, is a major part of my journey. The space I share with Phil has made a significant contribution to that.

I now know, and relish, the knowledge that these sessions with Phil are an opportunity to talk about spiritual ideas, to explore new insights and experiences, and to experience a special level of meeting with an other – and all this in addition to tremendous and tangible benefits on a physical level!

From Counsellor to Fellow Traveller

My relationship with Bryce began as a formal helping relationship. As I have described in *My Awakening,* Bryce was the guest facilitator on my six month counselling course, and, as he was describing the criteria for recognising that someone might be traumatised, I was shocked to realise that I fulfilled all of them – even though I thought I was managing everything pretty well. This was almost 12 months after Neil died and just after the relationship with Paul (CPN) had ended, so I turned down his first offer of help. However, after a few weeks I knew I did need help and that I really wasn't functioning as well as I thought I was. I realised that I needed (wanted?) to take further the beginnings of what I had learned with Paul. I just couldn't 'put the genie back in the bottle' even if I'd wanted to, and by this time I wasn't sure that I did – 'ignorance is bliss' might have its attractions on some level but once the dam was breached there was no going back. So when he offered his help again, I accepted – with trepidation.

I could no longer ignore what I was feeling – at peril of survival – and this formal helping aspect of our relationship continued for 19 months. As *My Awakening* illustrates, it was an eventful and completely life-changing time for me. It was also the time when I first encountered the idea that it is the relationship which is crucial in a helping situation. I began to learn how much the person is the 'instrument' for help far more than any skills or academic understanding. These, naturally, inform the work but they are not the work, pretty much like rituals support and inform the work on the spiritual journey, they are not the journey.

Bryce accompanied me through my darkest days and enabled me to put the pieces back together – albeit in a very different order. It was his presence, his acceptance, his ability to simply **be** with me that enabled me to look at my own inner world, to face the demons and the patterns that held me and which gave me such pain and anguish. This aspect of my journey has been so critical in my awakening and in my transformation that I feel I cannot emphasise it enough.

His intuition, experience and understanding of the journey enabled him to offer me suggestions for steps forward: strategies to use; people it might be useful to meet (Lyn, Maggie); places to visit (particularly Rievaulx Abbey); books to read; poetry to read and write; music to listen to. And always with a choice: my choice what I took on and what I didn't; my freedom to say whether something fitted for me or not.

He reached a point in the counselling process where he identified a big shift; he noted that he was now my teacher or guide rather than my counsellor/helper. This was a turning point. Although I still needed support, the main focus shifted from the past towards learning more and more about the journey I was on, *this moment*. Not long after this our formal relationship came to an end as I began PCMC.

At about this time I began to take on the role of proof reader for some of his work. This began another phase of our relationship, giving me both the opportunity to bring myself into a peer relationship with him and to gain yet more insight into trusting myself. I began very timidly offering changes and only rarely would I alter a sentence without checking with him first but it quickly became clear that Bryce trusted me in this far more than I trusted myself.

Trusting myself in this way challenged my deep seated belief that if I could do something then everybody else can do it as well as, if not better than, me. This lived in me as a form of put down of me; an inability to recognise that I do have certain gifts and skills that, perhaps, not everyone has. Gradually, because all my suggestions, alterations, and comments were described by Bryce as useful, accurate and insightful, I began to trust myself more, finally stepping into a full editor's role. So, here was the opportunity to extend my self-belief and my self-esteem. I thoroughly enjoy the work I do and relish the many thought-provoking and fascinating conversations we have around the various documents.

One day when the jaw injury I'd sustained through playing staff football was giving me a lot of trouble, I mentioned it to Bryce and he said he could 'do something' for that. This was my introduction into healing of a very different kind, adding yet another dimension to the relationship. In the healing sessions I received many visions, insights, understandings, in addition to the physical benefits of the healing. He encouraged me to work with the images; to reflect upon them and to talk about them. My understanding of how much the body holds – both from events or injuries in this life and from past lives – grew hugely and I began a process of releasing the tensions, the fear, the deep, deep memories that my body held.

As my need for therapeutic interventions lessened so my awareness of the necessity for a listening ear, someone with whom I could explore the increasing occurrence of 'out of this world' kinds of experiences, grew ever stronger. As my understanding of other worlds grew and as my 'whacky' experiences increased and became what seemed ever more strange, there were fewer and fewer people with whom I could talk about them. How many people, after all, would be able to hear about spirit journeys, about animal guides, about travelling in other realms, about my 'heretical' views from within the Anglican Church? In addition, I was very reticent about speaking out to 'just anybody' because if I did my anxiety was that I would be thought mad, or a fraud, or dangerous, or not fit to be kept as a friend – or all of these.

Our conversations thus began to move into a more overt exploration of other realms: spirit beings, elementals; healing; journeying; spiritual dimensions; the transpersonal; my relationship with God – nothing was off the radar in this area. Sometimes, my experiences were so new and so outside the norm that I struggled to find words to express what I felt or experienced. On these occasions he was often able to express the concept or the idea in a way that fitted for me and that took me a step further in my exploration. Not all my experiences could be described as all light and joy; there are darker times and darker places in which I am called to work, and it was just as important – if not more so – to have a place to talk about these too. This is incredibly affirming, challenging, supporting – sometimes all at once.

I have undertaken a number of journeys, both shamanic and physically travelling, all of which have been highly significant and awe-full. They have had considerable impact upon the way I view the world, upon how I choose to operate within the world, upon how I see myself and upon how I can continue to grow into who I was born to be, and upon what I discover to be my calling in other realms. As I have taken on different roles and tasks in these realms, it has been truly remarkable to have someone with whom I can share anything I choose of what I experience in those realms and in those worlds.

The fact that Bryce has been part of my journey in different ways almost since its very beginning is wonderful and is a great bonus – here is someone who knows the history, the shifts, the transformations, and all that it has taken for me to be where I am now and to be who I am.

SUMMARY

Becoming Who I Was Born To Be

"When we have been encouraged to be who we are – see what we see, know what we know, and act on our knowledge – we can find others like ourselves. And then together we can begin creating new worlds."

Carol Pearson, *Awakening the Heroes Within,* p281. HarperSanFrancisco, 1991.

正念
Mindfulness

To look consciously for something else; to choose deliberately to discover more, to explore, to move beyond the accepted norms and preconditions of our society and culture is a huge undertaking. It takes courage and determination and persistence – but it is worth it.

勇
Courage

希
Hope

The journey is for nothing less than gaining freedom: freedom to know my Self fully; freedom to live as a free spirit; freedom to move beyond any limiting messages I have from the moment I was born – and before. Freedom to **be** who I truly know myself to be. It is exciting, terrifying, ecstatic, exhilarating, daunting and liberating – often at the same

逍遥
Freedom

time. There are unanticipated consequences; dangers of a sense of isolation with fewer people to talk with about my experiences; there are challenges to take on; the unknown to be faced; the wondrous to behold; the darkness to be entered and faced.

Love

It is in those moments and places when I can allow every part of myself to be fully present that I experience the wonder of my being; freedom and transcendence. When I come from that place of heart openness and willingness to connect with my innermost being and with the powers of the universe then anything is possible.

Becoming who I was born to be is remembering and re-discovering my true nature, my sacredness, my connection to the universe, my place in the collective consciousness, the unique role I have been given and, crucially, to fulfil this role in relationship with others.

Intent

It has become ever clearer to me that, although my path is largely a solitary one, it has to be part of my being in the world too. It is in relationship that healing of self, other and universe can take place, and it is where the next steps forward in raising levels of consciousness can be explored and implemented. As I heal myself, I heal the universe; as each of us works towards healing ourselves, we heal the universe.

> "Let each become all that he was created capable of being; expand, if possible, to his full growth, and show himself at length in his own shape and stature, be these what they may."
>
> **Thomas Carlyle** in Zaleski & Kaufman, *Gifts of the Spirit,* p160. HarperSanFrancisco, 1998.

恕
Forgiveness

The quote above encapsulates so much of what I have endeavoured to express and holds the key for the way forward. As all the many interconnecting threads of my life and the lives of others on their journeys – on *our* journey – are woven together, we come to know more of our true nature and the wonderful potential we have. We are, indeed, all unique individuals, yet it is the 'music' we can make together that will enable us both to transform our own lives and contribute to the healing of our communities, the planet and the universe.

同情
Compassion

Honouring my journey, honouring my commitment to myself, honouring the people who have played a role, and integrating my past (rather than being controlled by it) are all hugely significant and important to me. Living the authentic life and being open to recognising those times when I am neither congruent nor authentic is also important; noticing these occasions, doing whatever is necessary and then moving on is a vital part of living the life that is mine.

Enabling my true Self, my soul if you will, to take on this calling is a lifetime's (and lifetimes') work – and it is the truest, most glorious and most demanding work there is. Enabling my soul, my deepest being, to find my authority, my own moral purpose and my own voice is the essence of *going soul-o*.

AFTERWORD

Into the Future

As this book was being prepared for printing in Spring 2010, Bryce Taylor died suddenly.

In the time since that shocking news, as I pause and think about my 'travels' with Bryce, I find that, amongst the deep grief, I am filled with joy and gratitude that I have been in relationship with him for over 18 years. In those years, as this book testifies, our connection shifted from client/counsellor to a mutual, collaborative and spiritual one. (Though I am not sure any relationship that is truly collaborative can be anything other than spiritual – even if that dimension is not overtly recognised or acknowledged.)

This is a time of great reflection upon that relationship – honouring, claiming and recognising what was. A time of remembering, of celebration, of tears, of sadness and joy, of awe at the journey travelled. And I am so thankful that I was given the honour and privilege to be asked to lead his funeral service.

It is a time of withdrawal to a degree in the sense of giving time and energy to the process of grief; a process that is exhausting in and of itself, so I am doing less of my usual day-to-day activities.

It is a time of revisiting what my role as editor has meant to me over the years, and for honouring and recognising the importance of that dimension of our relationship – to both of us. I have relished and delighted in the many conversations we have had in order to... clarify a sentence or two; expand upon an idea; find ways to link disparate ideas; suggestions for additions; simply to have discussions around the concepts with no direct input to the live document. I find I still reach for the phone – and then I remember.

It is also a time of coming to terms with the notion of travelling alone – without the 'witness' who has been present at so many critical and pivotal moments almost from the very beginning of my awakening.

As has often been the case, I very soon had an experience that turned things upside down and which challenged me to see things from a different perspective. In January this year (2010) I awoke the night after a weekend workshop around evolutionary consciousness knowing I needed to visit Auschwitz. It was clear to me that I had some work to do – in spiritual realms – around the events that took place at Auschwitz but I had no clarity about how this would manifest itself. What I did know was that the words *responsibility* and *redemption* were key. I was pretty sure it would be a powerful experience whatever the work I was called upon to do, so I arranged a city break to Krakow (with Auschwitz as a day visit) in April when I could spend a chunk of time with Bryce the day after I got back.

After Bryce's death a number of folk suggested I postpone the trip until later. I seriously considered it yet I knew it was important for me to be there that weekend, though I had no idea why I felt so strongly about it. So I went anyway and within two hours of arriving in Krakow I knew one reason why I was there at that particular time. I was in the magnificent – and very large – square in Krakow when I heard some haunting, moving religious singing and I was drawn to follow the sound. In St Mary's, one of the most important churches in the area, a service was taking place. I stayed. I was drawn by the people outside and by the enormous screen relaying the service within to those of us outside. I couldn't understand a word but it was really important that I was there.

I soon realised it was the funeral service of someone who was killed in April's plane crash in which the Polish president, his wife and many key people of the country all died. I later discovered that it was one of the Generals – the head of the Armed Services.

Suddenly and gently I was aware of my fellow guides – with Bryce. I am familiar with that feeling of having another entity within and with me; distinct yet connected; linked to me yet all over and everywhere; in one place and all places; personal and yet impersonal; individual yet part of everything and all that is. Yet in some ways this experience felt truly unique. For the first time, my cohort now included someone I have known so closely in embodied form. The rest of my cohort, with the exception of the Dongba priest (who I met in those brief yet powerful moments that night at the theatre in China), are only known to me in other realms.

We were playing a crucial role in that square. Our energy was holding all those who were grieving; supportive and yet it felt more than that. I can't find the words for the experience. It was amazing – our energy, our presence was important for holding those who were there, particularly for those outside the church. It is difficult to express the precise quality except that it was positive, healing and available to anyone and everyone whether they were aware of the concept and possibilities or not. Throughout the experiences and others that took place later in the day, I felt fully in touch with that sense of expansion, of stillness, of connection with all things and this stayed with me for the whole trip.

When we arrived at Auschwitz two days later I was initially surprised by the number of coaches in the car park. So many people and so much activity and chatter! Yet on entering the site there was a palpable shift in atmosphere, in consciousness. There were a few birds singing and there were a few wild flowers here and there, yet my overwhelming impression was of coldness, of 'hush', of something – something unspoken; something malevolent – hanging in the air.

In one of the first huts we visited, I felt a great sense of evil and, simultaneously, I felt rising within me a tremendously strong anger towards those who could perpetrate such atrocities. Yet almost in the same instant I was engulfed by a wave – a tsunami – of compassion, of understanding, which flooded away the anger, revulsion and hardness.

The day ended with a visit to Auschwitz 2 (Birkenau) where, after a brief tour, we were given an hour's free time. I walked to the Memorial at the end of the railway line to the crematoria and simply sat quietly to one side. I stayed there for the whole time I had available; aware of so much, reflecting on the many experiences of the day, crying at times, just 'being' at others. When it was time to return to the coach, I stood, turned away and then felt an incredibly strong impulse to look once more at the Memorial. As I gazed and soaked in the amazing, almost bizarre, calmness of the place I heard a clear message:

> "Your commission – should you choose to accept it – is to work with the perpetrators not the victims."

I had already received an insight concerning the victims early in the day: "You are not forgotten – you will never be forgotten". And it is crucial that this is the case; for them to be heard and recognised, yet here I was receiving a very unexpected commission.

I then remembered the experience in the hut where my anger, the sense of evil and revulsion had been immediately transformed into compassion and understanding. At that moment, gazing at the Memorial with my heart in my mouth, I knew that this was to be part of my role with my cohort: transforming anger and hate and all the 'stuff' that perpetuates such activities, allowing them to continue and to occur all over again.

This is at the ethereal, other realm level. It is not realistic to ask those still held by this to forgive, or to accept, or even, perhaps, to have compassion for the reasons why the perpetrators did what they did. The work needs to be done at the level of their very deepest being and essence – not at the level where such actions are manifested in the world.

Not long after the experience about the victims, I had sensed souls; lost and in great pain. They – in that state – knew what they had done but could not understand how come. Their pain is felt deep in their very core of being, their deepest essence – a level which many folk are unaware of when embodied.

My commission is around working with them to **release** them, to **free** them, to **enable redemption** to take place; to ease their pain. I simply stood there and accepted the commission. So simple yet so profound and such an awesome undertaking – or it certainly feels that way at the moment.

I had many amazing, moving, mind-blowing experiences at Auschwitz and Birkenau and, in the midst of them all, I knew I was not alone: not alone in the work I am called to undertake and not alone in my inner work either. I was so aware of Bryce throughout the day in a way that would not have been possible whilst he was alive.

In the event, therefore, my visit to Auschwitz turned out to be a time of preparation for the work rather than the work itself in three vital aspects:

1. I had to feel/experience the pain, appreciate the scale, and come to know something of the depth of the horrors, indignities and cruelty in order to work with it.

2. I was introduced both in Krakow and Auschwitz to the potential of working in other realms with Bryce as part of my cohort.

3. I must accept – and believe – that I do have the capacity to do this work and that I *am* able to undertake such commissions on my own. I was reminded, too, of a profound and significant journey I'd taken in November 2008 on completion of which Bryce had said, 'You don't need me for this anymore', and again in February 2009 when he spoke of the 'elegance' with which I undertook another powerful journey.

This visit to Krakow, Auschwitz and the ensuing commission feel pivotal in moving forward into the next stage of my life and my life's work. There is something about this being an opportunity to step more into my own autonomous power, to trust myself more and to listen to my own inner wisdom more; to step more fully into that person I know myself to be – that powerful, spiritually aware, connected and conscious being who is beautiful and who has a strong link to the Divine. A being, too, that has the capacity to influence in other realms on a far wider scale than any influence I might have in this one – whilst always knowing that I live in this realm and relate to folk in this realm and through this realm's mores.

So this period heralds the beginning of another phase: an opportunity to spread my wings and a chance to learn to give myself more affirmation and realistic appraisal of how and who I am.

But arguably above, and incorporating, all these is the opportunity to embrace yet more of *who I was born to be* and *going soul-o*.

The learning and the journey continue.

Bibliography

Jack Angelo, *Spiritual Healing: A Practical Guide to Hands-On Healing*. Godsfield Press, 2002.

Christopher M. Bache, *Dark Night, Early Dawn*. State University of New York, 2000.

Lyn Birkbeck, *Do it Yourself Life Plan Astrology*. Element Books, 2000.

William Bloom, *The Endorphin Effect*. Piatkus, 2001.

William Bloom, *Soulution: The Holistic Manifesto*. Hay House, 2005.

Joseph Campbell with Bill Moyers, *The Power of Myth*. Doubleday, 1988.

Joseph Campbell, *The Hero with a Thousand Faces* (2nd Edition). New World Library, 1968.

Joseph Campbell, *The Masks of God,* Volumes I-IV. Penguin Books, 1975.

Joseph Campbell, *Myths to Live By*. Souvenir Press, 1973.

Aldo Carotenuto, *The Spiral Way: A Woman's Healing Journey*. Inner City Books, 1986.

Carlos Casteneda, *The Art of Dreaming*. Element, 1993.

Carlos Casteneda, *A Separate Reality.* Penguin, Arkana, 1990.

Carlos Casteneda, *Journey to Ixtlan*. Penguin, Arkana, 1990.

Carlos Casteneda, *The Eagle's Gift*. Penguin, Arkana, 1992.

Bruce L Cathie, *The Energy Grid*. Adventures Unlimited Press, 1997.

Dr Gilbert Childs, *Understand your Temperament!* Sophia Books, 1995.

Dr Gilbert Childs, *Balancing Your Temperament*. Sophia Books, 1999.

Riane Eisler, *Chalice and the Blade*. Pandora, 1993.

Christina Feldman, *The Quest of the Warrior Woman: a path of healing, empowerment and transformation*. Thorsons, 1995.

Georg Feuerstein (Ed), *Enlightened Sexuality*. The Crossing Press, 1989.

Victor Frankl, *Man's Search for Meaning*. Washington Square Press, 1984.

Matthew Fox, *The Coming of the Cosmic Christ*. HarperSanFrancisco, 1988.

Anthony Giddens, *The Transformation of Intimacy*. Polity Press, 1995.

Rene Girard, *The Scapegoat*. The Johns Hopkins University Press, 1992.

Rene Girard, *Violence and the Sacred*. The Johns Hopkins University Press, 1986.

Ursula Le Guin, *The Earthsea Quartet*. Penguin, 1993.

Ursula Le Guin, *Searoad*. Flamingo, 1995.

Ursula Le Guin, *Tales from Earthsea*. Orion, 2002.

Arthur Guirdham, *We Are One Another*. Turnstone Press Ltd., 1982.

David Guy, *The Red Thread of Passion: Spirituality and the Paradox of Sex*. Shambala, 1999.

Hafiz, *The Gift: poems by Hafiz*; translator Daniel Ladinsky. Compass, 1999.

Andrew Harvey, *The Hidden Journey*. Bloomsbury, 1991.

James Hillman, *The Soul's Code*. Bantam, 1997.

Roger Housden, *Fire in the Heart*. Element, 1990.

Jean Houston, *The Search for the Beloved*. Tarcher and Putnam, 1987.

Sandra Ingerman, *Soul Retrieval*. HarperSanFrancisco, 1991.

Sandra Ingerman, *Shamanic Journeying*. Sounds True, 2006.

Sandra Ingerman & Hank Wesselman, *Awakening to the Spirit World: The Shamanic Path of Direct Revelation*. Sounds True, 2010.

Ma Jian, *Red Dust*. Anchor Books, 2002.

Sam Keen, *The Passionate Life: Stages of Loving*. Gateway Books, 1985.

Stephen Larsen, *The Shaman's Doorway*. Inner Traditions International, 1998.

Kriacos C Markides, *Homage to the Sun*. Penguin, Arkana, 1987.

Caitlin Matthews, *The Elements of the Goddess*. Elements, 1994.

Roger McGough, *Defying Gravity*. Penguin Books, 1993.

Kenneth Meadows, *Where Eagles Fly*. Element, 1995.

Arthur Mindel, *The Shaman's Body*. HarperSanFrancisco, 1993.

Dr Hiroshi Motoyama, *Karma & Reincarnation*. Piatkus, 1992.

Henri J M Nouwen, *The Way of the Heart*. Daybreak, Darton, Longman and Todd, 1990.

Carol S Pearson, *Awakening the Heroes Within*. HarperSanFrancisco, 1991.

M Scott Peck, *The Road Less Travelled*. Arrow, 1990.

Sylvia Brinton Perera, *Descent to the Goddess. A Way of Initiation for Women*. Inner City Books, 1981.

Sylvia Brinton Perera, *The Scapegoat Complex. Toward a Mythology of Shadow and Guilt*. Inner City Books, 1986.

Leo Rutherford, *Shamanic Path Workbook*. Arima Publishing, 2006.

Rainier Maria Rilke, *The Selected Poetry,* (Editor Stephen Mitchell). Picador, 1987.

John Snelling, *Way of Buddhism*. Thorson's, 2001.

Barbara Somers, *The Fires of Alchemy*. Archive Publishing, 2004.

Rudolf Steiner, *Secrets of the Threshold*. Anthroposophic Press, 1987.

Rudolf Steiner, *Four Temperaments*. Rudolf Steiner Publishing Co., 1944.

Charles Tart (Ed), *Altered States of Consciousness*. HarperSanFrancisco, 1990.

Bryce Taylor, *Helping People Change*. Oasis Press, 1995.

Bryce Taylor, *Archetypes, Myth, Story and Metaphor*. Oasis Press, 2002.

Bryce Taylor, *Working with Others* (6th Edition). Oasis Press, 2004.

Bryce Taylor & Nick Ellerby, *Discovering the Temperaments*. Oasis Press, 2004.

Angela Tilby, *Soul*. SPCK, 1994.

Alan Watts, *This Is It*. Rider, 1996.

John R Yungblut, *Shaping a Personal Myth to Live By*. Element, 1992.

Philip Zaleski & Paul Kaufman, *Gifts of the Spirit*. HarperSanFrancisco, 1998.